"Crying out its importance to a world made hectic by a crush of priorities, its message is a simple one, told in an unaffected style that reflects the cadence of prairie life."
—*Iowa Woman*

# Nothing to Do but Stay
## My Pioneer Mother

An extraordinary, highly acclaimed reading experience for all ages

"Told with warmth and humor . . . This is not an exercise in nostalgia, but a truthful portrait of a not so distant time when ingenuity and determination were the foundations of an austere but satisfying life."
—*Women Library Workers Journal*

"Vivid and loving snapshots of growing up on a frontier homestead."
—*Self*

"Delightful . . . superior work . . . Carrie Young selects details that invest her narrative of even simple occurrences in her family's life, such as a community gathering to eat ice cream on the Fourth of July, with a sense of freshness and adventure."

*—Western American Literature*

"Any whining yuppie who thinks a rough day of work means spending 12 hours in front of a spreadsheet needs to read this book. . . . Many of us who live in a world of desk work, take-out food, and cleaning services are in fact the grandchildren of strong, brave farm women like Carrine Gafkjen Berg, for whom a Thanksgiving dinner spent with friends was the pinnacle of happiness. It gives one pause."

*—Utne Reader*

"This thin, pleasant volume, with its family photographs and sketches of eccentric Norwegians, is a paean to the 'original pioneer women.' "

*—Belles Lettres*

ALSO BY CARRIE YOUNG
*The Wedding Dress*

# Nothing to Do but Stay

## MY PIONEER MOTHER

# Carrie Young

A LAUREL TRADE PAPERBACK
Published by
Dell Publishing
a division of
Bantam Doubleday Dell Publishing Group, Inc.
1540 Broadway
New York, New York 10036

Six of the essays in this collection appeared originally as follows: "The Education of a Family," *Missouri Review* 9, no. 3 (1986); "Prairie Cook" and "Thanks for the Last" (under the title "A Scandinavian Thanksgiving in North Dakota"), *Gourmet*, copyright © 1983 by *Gourmet*, reprinted by permission; "The Last Turkey," *Minneapolis Star Tribune* Sunday Magazine (1986); an excerpt from "Ole and Anna" (under the title "The Crazy Christmas Tree"), *American West* (1986); "A Fourth of July in North Dakota" (under the title "A Fourth of July on the Prairies"), *Kansas Quarterly* 20, no. 4 (1988).

ISBN: 0-440-50523-2

Reprinted by arrangement with University of Iowa Press

Printed in the United States of America

Published simultaneously in Canada

August 1993

10  9  8  7  6  5  4  3  2  1

FFG

FOR MY PARENTS

Carrine Gafkjen Berg
1879–1962

Sever K. Berg
1881–1964

# 1

## The Education of a Family

*My pioneer mother was wild for education. She fer-*vently believed that young people given enough schooling and using the brains they were born with could rise above themselves as far as they wanted to go, the sky the limit. She herself, with no formal education of any kind, had managed to lead a remarkable life characterized from end to end with vision and courage. The daughter of Norwegian immigrants, she had supported herself from the time she was a very young girl and in her middle twenties had struck out alone to homestead on the North Dakota prairies. Almost a decade later, after she had become a secure woman of property and at an age when most women of her time had been declared spinsters, she married and raised six children.

Born in Norway's Hallingdal valley, my mother, Carrine Gafkjen, was three when she came with her parents in the early 1880s to a southern Minnesota farm. She attended, on and off, a one-room country school, but after several years her parents withdrew her permanently to help on the farm. They were, on the other hand, strict Lutherans; they taught her to read Norwegian so that she could study her catechism and be confirmed in the Norwegian Lutheran Church. My mother memorized every word in the one-hundred-page catechism. Fifty years later she could recite it by rote.

Sent at fifteen to "work out" in the home of a Sauk Centre family, she lived on the same street as Sinclair Lewis. Then a boy of nine or ten, Harry, as she called him, one day came to her back door and pressed a handsome piece of watermelon on her. She wanted to eat it but she didn't dare; she thought Harry was, as usual, up to something. After he left she threw it away. (When thirty-five years later she learned that Sinclair Lewis had received the Nobel Prize, she regretted not having eaten that watermelon. "I suppose it would have been all right," she said.)

My mother soon moved to Minneapolis where she worked as a cook and housekeeper for the next ten years, saving almost everything she earned, always with the sin-

*My pioneer mother shortly before going out to North Dakota to homestead. From the author's collection.*

gle-minded intention of homesteading. In the spring of 1904, when she was twenty-five—a handsome dark-eyed woman wearing a great billowing hat, her slender figure hidden under a long black coat with leg-o'-mutton sleeves —she boarded a train for northwestern North Dakota. In the frontier town of Williston, she rented a horse and buckboard and drove thirty miles north where the prairies lay 2,130 feet above sea level and thousands of acres, most of them still unclaimed, rolled from horizon to horizon. Here she staked out her 160-acre homestead. She had a tiny one-room cabin erected and lived there alone for the required six months, every night barring her door against the coyotes. Her only furniture was a potbellied stove (with a surface large enough to boil a pan of water), a shakedown bed, a table, and a chair. Once a week she walked five miles to the Little Muddy Creek to wash her clothes and to bring back enough water to boil for drinking. She lived on potatoes and salt. She hired a man with a breaking plow and four oxen to turn over the required number of acres of virgin soil.

When autumn came, she went to the federal land office in Williston and "proved up," the term the homesteaders used for submitting proof that they had fulfilled all of the conditions of the Homestead Act. She exercised the option of paying $1.25 in cash per acre for her land. One year later, she received the patent from Washington, D.C., dated September 26, 1905. Still in my family, it is a magnificent piece of parchment, on which my mother's name and the description of her land are executed in large round calligraphy. The document is signed in a small nondescript scrawl, *T. Roosevelt.*

During the winter for the next eight years, my mother worked as a housekeeper for a well-to-do farm family in the eastern part of the state, and in the summer she returned to her homestead to cook for one of the large threshing crews operating in the territory. She had the remainder of her land plowed and rented it out on crop shares. With the income from her crops, along with her wages, she was able after a few years to buy another quarter section of land near her homestead. At thirty, she had become a woman of means, the owner of 320 acres of rich North Dakota farmland, free and clear with no mortgages or other encumbrances.

My father, Sever Berg, had homesteaded, too, in another township. My mother met him one summer when he was firing the steam engine on the threshing rig for which she cooked. When she heard the familiar Halling accent and learned that his parents had grown up in the same county in Norway as her own, she knew that my father and she had been destined to find each other halfway across the world, and she hesitated no longer; she married him before the year was out in 1912. They decided to sell my father's homestead and build up their farm on my mother's land, which lay pleasingly higher in the sun and had richer, more productive soil.

At thirty-four, my mother was afraid that her childbearing years had passed. Not to worry. She bore six children in nine years. First my sisters Bernice and Florence, then my brother Norman, then in rapid succession Gladys and Frances and me. All six of us completed elementary school in a one-room country schoolhouse down the road from our farm.

Because I was the youngest of the six, I recall our process of education as a sort of stepping-stone marathon. It begins with my first memory at the age of four saying good-bye to my two oldest sisters as they left home to go to high school and ends with my own graduation from college seventeen years later in 1944. During all of these years I followed in the footsteps of my sisters and brother, hopping from stone to stone as, urged on by my mother, we tried to complete our education in the years before, during, and after the Dust Bowl.

My oldest sisters, Barney and Florence, went in tandem through grade school because Barney was late in starting. During a raging North Dakota blizzard when she was five, she had suffered an attack of appendicitis, and before my parents could get her on a train to the nearest surgeon, who was three hundred miles across the state in Grand Forks, peritonitis had set in. It took Barney a year to recover from her illness, and by then Florence was old enough to start school, too.

They both finished off their grammar school in a fast six years, however, because our country schoolteachers had a habit of arbitrarily letting pupils they considered smarter than others skip entire grades. One reason for this practice might have been self-serving; if the teacher saw an opportunity to make her days less harried by combining several students into the same grade, she took it. Whatever the reason, perhaps because Barney was older and Florence was the quintessential quick-witted child prodigy, when they were thirteen and eleven they had been promoted out of the eighth grade and were ready for high school.

There was no question in my mother's mind that they *would* go to high school, even though the closest accredited four-year high school was thirty miles away at Williston and despite the fact that higher education was frowned upon in our farm community. Most of the parents took the position that it served only to spoil young people and, even more dangerous, it lured them away from farm life.

My father could have gone along with this theory easily enough if it hadn't been for my mother, who convinced him that it was old-fashioned thinking. This was the right approach to take with my father because he loved "progress," and once he had been persuaded that educating his children was progress, he was all for it. My parents went to Williston the week before school started in the fall of 1927 and rented a sleeping room with cooking privileges in a private residence for Barney and Florence, at the same time enrolling them in Williston High School.

During the early autumn months my father drove to Williston every Friday evening to bring my sisters home for the weekend; but by the middle of November they had to stay in town week after week because the snow-covered country roads were frequently impassable. There was still only a dirt road to Williston; U.S. Highway 85, which in a few years would bisect the Midwest from Mexico to Canada and come within two miles of our farm, had not yet reached northwestern North Dakota. When the Christmas holidays came, my father shoveled his way out of dozens of snowdrifts to get the girls home. He started out in his 1927 Ford sedan early on a Saturday morning, and the three of them didn't get home until midnight. My mother stood for hours in an upstairs window that night, looking for lights across the prairies. When she sighted the automobile lights five miles away, she tracked them from snowdrift to snowdrift, hour after hour, until they made the turn on the last mile toward home. Then she went down to the kitchen and put the potatoes on to boil.

My parents decided they would try to rent a house in town for the remainder of the school year; my mother would live in town with us five girls, and my father would

*Nothing to Do but Stay*

stay out on the farm with my brother Norman and look after the livestock. They counted themselves lucky to find a small two-story house and, one cold bright day when the roads were clear, my father loaded into his truck much of the furniture from our farmhouse, including the Clarendon upright piano, and moved us in to Williston. The first Monday after New Year's my mother took my sisters Fran and Gladys to the city elementary school and enrolled them in the first and third grades. When noon came, Barney and Florence came running home and found a hot lunch waiting for them. Florence sang out, "Now all our troubles are over!"

Not quite. My father came in from the country the following Friday evening and found two men from the Williston school board waiting in the living room for him. The men informed him that the board had met in special session the previous evening and had concluded that since our farm was located in another township my father must pay tuition, amounting to hundreds of dollars, if Gladys and Fran were to continue to attend elementary school in the city. My father turned white and showed them to the door. He was already paying tuition for the older girls to attend high school; the additional fee would be prohibitive. The next morning he took Barney and Florence back to their rented sleeping room, and then he piled all of our furniture into the truck and moved us back to the farm. That night, with packing boxes sitting all over the kitchen,

*The Education of a Family*

my mother made us pancakes on the coal range for supper. She said that it was good to be home.

My father never again mentioned this incident. He always believed that in no-win situations what is done is done and the faster one forgets about it the better.

My parents would have done well if they could have blotted out the winter of 1928 entirely. My mother had no more than emptied the packing boxes before my father came down with rheumatic fever, probably brought on by the strain of many hours of heavy lifting in subzero temperatures. The only doctor in the territory who would make house calls was an old man named Dr. Wicklund who lived in the small hamlet of Wildrose, twenty-five miles to the north of us. My mother waylaid the mailman and had him send a telegram to Dr. Wicklund, and a day or two later he came out in his one-horse buggy on sled runners. Dr. Wicklund was all one color: charcoal. His horse and buggy were charcoal, as were his suit of clothes and his hair and mustache. He pulled up a kitchen chair to the side of the bed and took my father's pulse with one hand while holding a heavy gold watch in the other. My mother loved Dr. Wicklund. In the winter of 1921 he had driven from Wildrose in a blinding snowstorm to deliver my sister Fran, no worse for the wear, who weighed twelve pounds and who was, according to my mother's distraught calculations, a month overdue. Fran was the only one of us not delivered by a midwife. Dr. Wicklund had brought both

Fran and me, in our early years, through pneumonia. Sitting now at my father's bedside, he shook his head as he examined my father's tender swollen joints. Then he went into the kitchen and told my mother, who was making him beefsteak and eggs against the long trip home, that the only cure for my father was prolonged bed rest until the fever had ridden itself out. He gave my mother a large bottle of wintergreen oil with which to massage my father's joints.

My father stayed in bed the remainder of the winter. My mother spent many hours a day out at the barn, milking the cows and feeding and watering the other livestock and poultry. When she came in with the pails of milk, she would turn the DeLaval cream separator, then take it apart and wash it along with the breakfast dishes. Then she would rub my father's joints with the wintergreen oil. I was the only child not in school, and I would sit on the foot of the bed watching my mother. I knew that after a certain length of time the smell of wintergreen would make her nauseated and she would find an excuse to hurry into the kitchen, but she never let on to my father that it made her ill. Even today, if I catch the faint scent of wintergreen, I instantly see my father in his bed in the winter of 1928.

My mother said, many years afterward, that this was the only time in all of their married life that she saw any visible sign that my father was worried about anything—and this included all of the Dust Bowl years. She said this was the only time in his life he couldn't get up out of bed and put on his pants—which for him was the criterion for being able to handle anything that came along. He lay in bed and fidgeted, worrying that if something happened to Barney and Florence in Williston he couldn't get there, and then he would make my mother mail them another twenty-dollar bill. After a few weeks my sisters wrote, "Stop sending money. We don't know what to do with it."

When spring break-up came the last week in March and the snowdrifts began to diminish, my father's fever started to subside, too, and by the middle of April he was well enough to harness up his draft horses and plow his fields and seed his crops. Contrary to the dire predictions of a few community soothsayers that he would never be strong again, my father had no lasting aftereffects of his illness, nor did he ever have rheumatic fever again.

In 1928—with the Dust Bowl still in the future—my parents were what was commonly termed as "well fixed." Their wheat crops in the fifteen years they had been married had given them the means to buy another half section of land, giving them 640 acres in all, debt free. Safely stowed away in the State Bank at Appam, the small town five miles to the north of us, were substantial cash savings —more than enough to send my two older sisters through a state teachers college in a few years.

When I was three months past five years old, in the autumn of 1928, I started first grade. I was so tiny I looked more like three than five, but it had been so lonesome at home the previous winter I could scarcely stand it; I whined and nagged until my mother consented to let me go. In hindsight, she acknowledged that it was a mistake. After my first month in school, the teacher—a motherly soul I adored—became ill and had to leave. The second teacher after a few weeks began showing pregnant and had to get married. The third teacher was a six-foot giantess who instantly resented me because she didn't think she should be required to play nursemaid to a five-year-old when she already had ten legitimate pupils in all eight grades.

To make matters worse, as winter came on I caught a terrible cold, but instead of keeping me at home my mother let me go to school, with instructions that I was not to go out to play during the lunch hour and that Gladys must stay in to keep me company. The giantess didn't care for this arrangement at all; she wanted her privacy during the lunch hour. She told Gladys to go on out to play and she'd take care of me. Not a middle child for nothing, Gladys stood her ground like a trooper, but she was no match for the Amazon and she had her walking papers in a hurry. Alone with the teacher, I wailed in terror, whereupon she took me by the wrist and hurled me across the room. A wrenching pain went through my wrist as I flew across the floor, which was always slippery with the red cleaning compound used to soak up the dirt. The teacher told me to sit at my desk and she didn't want to hear another peep out of me. I knew she meant business. I sat frozen at my desk until my father came to take us home from school. By then my wrist was swollen to twice its size. My mother bandaged it, and I stayed home for a month. Every night I cried myself to sleep at the thought of going back to school.

My mother took the position that I was the one who had nagged her to go in the first place and this is what had happened and now it was up to me. She tossed her head (my mother was the most convincing head tosser I have ever known) and declared that she didn't care one way or another whether I went back to school. Five years old and I had a horrendous "free choice" hanging over me. I thought that if only she would say I *must* go back I could throw a tantrum and cry that no one could ever make me; or if she would just say that I *couldn't* go back, I could protest mildly but not enough to change her mind. As it turned out, the teacher herself made the decision for me. One day Norman, Gladys, and Fran came home from school and reported that the giantess had remarked with a satisfied smile, in front of the entire school, that she was certain she'd "never see baby sister again."

That did it. The next day I went back. When the Amazon saw me walk in, she shrugged and lifted her eyebrows. She set me on my desk and pulled off my overshoes.

In my second year, we had a teacher whose temper was so legendary it had followed her from school to school across the western states. Why the school board hired her is a mystery—except that finding teachers who were willing to take over a one-room school in a state where a winter temperature of zero is considered mild was an exercise in catch-as-catch-can. My father was as much to blame as anyone; he was president of the school board at the time. I think he chose a schoolteacher in the same way he chose a Christmas tree: they all looked alike to him so might as well take the first one at hand.

Miss Washburn was in her middle thirties and skinny, with a mottled complexion that looked as if it might have been buffeted by too many western winds. The first day of school we sat on edge, waiting every minute for the famous temper to erupt. It didn't. Days went by, then weeks, then months—September, October, and November. The consensus on the playground was that the temper rumors were false: there was no temper. My brother Norman and the other older boys relaxed and began to cut up a bit. One day Miss Washburn looked up from her desk and caught them throwing spitballs. Like a reflex action, every object on her desk flew across the room. She wheeled in her chair and along came the blackboard erasers and the chalk. "Class dismissed!" she shrieked. We fled from the room.

Fifteen minutes later, when she rang the bell, we didn't know whether to risk going in or take for the road. When we cautiously stepped over the threshold, we saw that the schoolroom was shipshape; the only sign of a holocaust was some chalkdust on the floor. And teacher was wearing a saintly smile.

In fact, the temper turned out to be the least of Miss Washburn's faults. Much worse was her habit of soaking up the heat. The schoolroom was heated by a round-bellied stove that stood in a corner. It burned coal, buckets of which the older boys carried in several times during the day from the coal bin behind the building. The stove had great aluminum arms wrapped around it that, when opened wide, created a shield at each side of the stove from which the heat could bounce off and rebound out into the schoolroom. When the stove was not in use, or in the unlikely circumstance that the room became too warm, the arms could be closed around the stove and fastened.

On below-zero days Miss Washburn stood in front of the stove, textbook in hand, and with the other hand she pulled the aluminum arms of the stove around her to encase herself in a cozy shell, while her pupils sat at their desks turning numb. When she saw that our fingers could no longer hold our pencils, she'd say, "All right, children.

Run around the desks for five minutes and get the circulation up!"

Lunch didn't do much to heat us up, either. She made us store our lunchpails in the cloakroom, which was unheated; frozen peanut butter sandwiches and ice water were standard fare that winter. Just about the nicest aspect of Miss Washburn was that at the end of the year she took her chill and her fabled temper and continued her trek eastward.

Norman had moved on to high school by the beginning of my third year in country school; there were only we three younger sisters left, and we got lucky. The new teacher was a blond buxom young woman with a placid warm-blooded nature; she threw the aluminum arms of the stove open to share the heat. We loved her instantly. She simultaneously lisped and fluttered her eyelashes, which enchanted us. Every day after noon recess she read aloud to us from a storybook. She read *The Bobbsey Twins at Uncle Frank's Ranch, Five Little Peppers and How They Grew,* and the *Just So Stories.* This was a treat so rare we could scarcely believe it. We sat with our cheeks in our hands, entranced. After my grim first and second grades, the three years in which Miss Helm taught seemed like an idyll. Not only did we love her, but she also had two boyfriends who loved her, and we followed her romantic involvements avidly. Both of her suitors were farmers. We quickly noticed that she didn't much care for one, that she kept him more or less as a backup, but that she was crazy about the other one.

During the week, Miss Helm boarded with a farm family who lived a half mile down the road from the school, and on weekends she went home to her parents in the next township. Her boyfriends took turns coming for her on Friday evenings shortly after school was dismissed; when one was busy in the fields, the other would come. When the boy she didn't fancy came for her, she always insisted that they give my sisters and me a lift home. She just wouldn't take no for an answer. "Now you girls just hop in the back seat," she'd say graciously. "There's no reason in the world you should walk a mile and a half home when we are going right past your place."

On the other hand, when the boy she was wild about came to fetch her, she climbed into the car with him, talking baby talk as she lisped madly and fluttered her eyelashes, and the two of them would roar off into the sunset, leaving my sisters and me straggling down the road in the dust. We didn't mind a bit. We decided we'd have done the same thing under the circumstances.

Only one incident marred the pleasant three years of Miss Helm's tenure. It was so bizarre that it defies explanation, and after it was over we did not hold it against her. One winter day of her last year, when we came in from noon recess the first thing that caught our eyes was a sentence that Miss Helm had written in her large perfect round penmanship across the top of the front blackboard. What startled us, even before we read the words, was that she had used a brilliant purple iridescent chalk that we had not seen before. The message, glaring eerily down on us, read: Any Pupil Who Breaks the Rules Must *Face the Consequences*!

The last three words were underlined with a spooky light lavender chalk, and the exclamation point was shadow-lined with it. A thin knife of apprehension zig-zagged through me. I looked at the other children. Their mouths were slightly open, and they looked as if they'd seen a ghost. Miss Helm had a rather strange secretive look in her eyes but gave no explanation for the sentence. At recess her twelve pupils huddled together on the play-ground and asked each other, "What are *Consequences*, and what is it like to *Face* them?" No one knew. What had we done to deserve this? No one knew. There had been no discipline problem because all of the cutups had gradu-ated the previous year; we thought everything was going along just fine. Someone suggested we ask our parents. Yes, that was a good idea. No, someone else said, maybe these *Consequences* that have come up tell more about us than we want our parents to know, so we'd best keep quiet about it. That's right, another child said, and be-sides, they'd say what was all the fuss about just a piece of writing on the blackboard. Well, *they* hadn't seen the color of the chalk.

The sentence hung there for weeks like an angry purple cloud that might descend and swallow us at any moment. The first day that Miss Helm had washed the blackboard, we thought, aha, now she'll wash off the sentence, too. But no, she only washed *up* to the sentence, carefully leaving it intact. We took to shading our eyes so that we could read everything that was placed on the blackboard except the purple sentence. We could see that this irritated Miss Helm, but she could say nothing or she would have had to break her mysterious silence.

Retribution came in a strange and wonderful way on a balmy afternoon toward the end of spring break-up. The county superintendent of schools, whose office was in Williston, made it a habit of visiting every rural school in the county at least once or twice a year—usually in the fall and again in the spring. She was a no-nonsense woman who resembled Eleanor Roosevelt, right down to the Enna Jettick shoes. She always wore a loose-fitting mannish suit and a very large hat. By design, her visits were totally impromptu; she obviously felt that the only way she could learn how the schools were being operated was to drop in unexpectedly.

On this unusually warm April day, when the last patches of snow were melting in the ditches, the superintendent came driving down the road in her Model A black coupe so quietly that Miss Helm, who was absorbed at her desk, didn't hear her. We heard her, all right; we had heard her coming a mile away. Miss Helm had flung the windows open for the first time that spring to let in the sweet smell of earthy things thawing in the sun. Unlike city children who went to sleep and woke up to traffic noise, we were so sensitive to any sound that intruded on the silence of the prairie that we could hear a motor five minutes before we saw it.

As we heard the automobile approach, we cautiously craned our necks to look out of the window and knew instantly who it was; the black coupe was unmistakable. The room was so quiet we could hear each other breathe. We heard the car turn into the schoolyard, and then the stealthy squeak of a car door opening, but not closing; the venerable superintendent had years of training in sneak attack. The teacher, engrossed at her desk, heard nothing. It seemed like an eternity before the peremptory knock on the door broke the silence like a gunshot. Miss Helm jumped a foot. She looked out of the window and saw the telltale black coupe. She glanced swiftly around the room to see that everything was in order, and then whirled around to check the blackboard. Her eyes lit on the dreadful purple sentence. Her face went a brilliant anguished vermilion. She didn't hesitate a moment. She seized an eraser, reached up, and swept the awful statement from the blackboard and out of our lives.

◆

Later that spring of 1931, my mother reached a major landmark in the education of her children: she saw her two oldest daughters graduate from high school. We did the farm chores early in the evening so we could drive the thirty miles into Williston in time for the graduation ceremony. It was a proud moment for my mother as she watched my sisters in their pastel summer dresses with flowing cape sleeves pass under the traditional arch of lilac boughs to receive their diplomas. My mother was already bustling with plans for their entering Valley City State Teachers College in the fall. They had been accepted for the advanced two-year curriculum there which would qualify them to teach in any elementary school in North Dakota.

In the coming summer months, however, the family fortunes changed drastically. The drought years had begun in earnest: my parents had their second crop failure in a row. On top of that, the State Bank of Appam suddenly closed its doors on all of their money. My father came home from town that day and walked into the kitchen. He had a strange look in his eyes, but he was laughing.

"The bank busted," he said, and looked hard at my mother. She shook her head and turned sharply away.

My father had a four-thousand-dollar life insurance policy that he had taken out as a very young man and on which he had paid the premiums for thirty-three years. He cashed it in for less than half of its face value to send

Barney and Florence to college. The last several months of the second year were touch and go. Florence, whose natural talents lay in many directions, was a clever hairstylist and had learned finger waving on her own, which was the current hair-setting rage, and she earned all of her and Barney's incidental expenses by coiffing the other young women in the dormitory. My mother managed to come up with their remaining expenses with what she could glean from her sales of cream and butter.

When we started the three-hundred-mile automobile trip to Valley City on a bright June morning in 1933 to see my older sisters receive their Standard diplomas at spring commencement, my mother was radiant with relief; she thought she had just gone over the tallest hurdle in the process of educating her children. She expected that both Barney and Florence would get teaching jobs in the fall, and the plan was that they would save their money and get enough ahead so that both could contribute something toward sending Norman to the University of North Dakota to study engineering when he finished high school in a couple of years.

My mother's relief was short-lived. We had no more than arrived home from Valley City when Florence—the perennial child prodigy—received a letter from the teachers college informing her that the business office had belatedly taken note of the astounding fact that she was only seventeen years old and still a minor, and therefore, of course, she could not receive certification for another year.

What is more, as the summer wore on it began to look as if even Barney was not going to find a teaching job. The dreadful possibility loomed that both she and Florence would have to remain at home; job openings of any kind were rapidly becoming nonexistent. The only solution my mother could see was that they go on to college to get their degrees so that they could get better-paying positions teaching high school and therefore would be able to help us younger children as we came up. But harvesttime rolled around, proving what everyone already knew, that there was no wheat crop for the fourth year in a row.

My mother was desperate. Here she was, she pointed out, a woman of property; she should be able to borrow some money. If there was any word in the English language she hated, it was "mortgage." But for her children's education she would do anything, and one hot windy day in August she walked into the Citizens National Bank of Williston and requested a loan of a thousand dollars. As collateral, she offered 320 acres of the most productive land in Williams County. The president of the bank told her, in the most high-handed manner, that even if she owned all of the farmland in the entire state of North Dakota he wouldn't lend her a thousand dollars.

When she emerged from the bank that day my mother was angrier than I had ever seen her. She was not a swearing woman, so she uttered the worst word she could bring herself to say: *"Stygging!"* Nasty fellow.

Not until years later did my mother realize that this was one of the luckiest days of her life. What she couldn't have known on that summer morning in 1933 was that six more crop failures in a row were coming up and never in any of those years would she have been able to meet the mortgage payments. She would have lost her homestead land as surely as she stood in the bank that day putting it up as security.

And there was, as it happened, another way. A teaching vacancy at the last moment turned up in one of the four country schools in our township, and it was offered to Barney. She would live at home where she would have no expenses, Barney said, and she would contribute her entire salary of sixty dollars a month toward sending Florence to the University of North Dakota; when Florence obtained her degree after two years, she could teach in high school and send Norman to college. It seemed like a fine solution.

Norman and Gladys were now in Williston High School; Fran and I were the only siblings left in country school. Barney hadn't been offered our home school, however, but a more distant one two and a half miles from our farm. Fran and I could have transferred to her school because it was in our township, but Barney thought she was going to have enough problems teaching the neighbor children without having her little sisters in the classroom to boot. In fact, she was so nervous about her first year of teaching that she replaced her regular eyeglasses with a pair of pince-nez from the mail order in the hope of adding some dignity to her nineteen years.

In the early autumn months, Barney drove the family Dodge to her school and Fran and I walked in the opposite direction to ours. By Thanksgiving, however, so much snow already covered the ground that Barney could no longer drive; the road to her school wasn't even graded. It was only a dirt trail. My father had to take her in the truck —then hurry home to take Fran and me to school. After a few weeks of this my father rebelled at maintaining full-time bus service in opposite directions on the worsening winter roads; he made Fran and me transfer to Barney's school after the winter holidays.

The most desolate school in the township, Freeman School Number One sat on a windswept hill at the edge of the vast Freeman ranch, one of the few full-scale cattle ranches left in the territory. Whoever built Freeman School Number One was either an incurable optimist or had never lived through a North Dakota winter; all six of its windows were on the west wall. Throughout the long winter months the harsh northwest winds blowing down from Canada caught and mercilessly battered them. The rattle was deafening. The township couldn't afford storm windows; icy air whistled through the corners, creating a draft that moved the papers on our desks.

Unlike the three other township schools—which had sensible heating stoves in the classroom—this building had been fancied up with a furnace in the basement. A warm air register about four feet square was built into the floor in the center of the room. Whenever pupils became too chilled at their desks, they would raise their hands and ask permission to stand on the register. On days the thermometer sank to twenty degrees below, the entire school population of fourteen jostled on it. It was necessary for Barney to go to the basement periodically to stoke the furnace with coal. When she returned discipline had gone haywire, erasers and chalk flying through the air. Even the pince-nez had difficulty restoring order.

By the end of January my father's truck equipped with heavy tire chains could no longer plow through the long stretch of country trail to Barney's school; no motor vehicle's axle could clear the drifts of snow under which the prairie lay like a frozen Siberia. The winter was already showing signs of being one of the worst in the region's history. My father had spent the entire month shoveling off the roads, and he was exhausted. He loved to shovel snow; he considered it a challenge. He had always been able to keep the road to our home school open, but it was partially graded. The two-and-a-half miles of trail to Freeman School Number One, he finally had to admit, were too much for him.

My father still had a team of old draft horses with which he had worked his fields before he acquired his first tractor. Queen and Nancy had been put out to pasture years ago and were about sixteen years old. They were bay mares, fat and sassy from having stood idle for so long. My father pulled down from high on the barn wall their dusty harnesses he had never again expected to use. He found some old horseshoes in his tin blacksmith shop and shod the mares. This, fortunately, was a skill he possessed; he had run a smithy in his early homesteading days in which he sharpened plowshares and shoed horses for his neighbors.

He harnessed up Queen and Nancy and hitched them to his old box sled. My mother placed numerous quilts in the bottom of the sled and wrapped her heavy flatirons in towels and put them in with the quilts to warm our feet. Barney, Fran, and I sat on the floor of the sled with more quilts over our heads, and my father stood up in the sled and drove the team. The snow was hard and the sled runners skimmed on top of it, but the horses broke through much of the time.

It took Queen and Nancy ninety minutes to get us to school. The three of us sat under the quilts listening to my father talk to the horses. There wasn't much talk. Only one word. "QVEEN! QVEEN!" Over and over again. Nancy

*Nothing to Do but Stay*

had always been willing to pull more than her weight, and Queen had been the laggard. After half a dozen years of standing fallow, Queen still remembered that Nancy would do her work for her if she hung back.

When we reached the school, my father would help Barney get the furnace going, and then he would sit in the basement by the furnace for a while after school was in session to thaw himself out before he started back. When he got home, he would unhitch the horses and put them in the barn and then take a sledgehammer and break the ice in the water tank so that he could water the horses and let the cows out to drink. Then he would grain the horses and go in the house to eat his lunch. At two o'clock it was time to hitch up the horses again and come for us.

Even on Saturday my father got no surcease because this was the day he and my mother went to Williston with provisions for Norman and Gladys, who were sharing a small apartment while attending high school. U.S. Highway 85 had now been completed. My father kept his automobile at the farm of a nephew who lived along the highway. He and my mother would take the team of horses there and then drive the car to Williston. This was an all-day trip in itself. And on Sunday it was church— another mile and back for Queen and Nancy.

By the first of March the horses were still holding up remarkably well, but my father was flagging. Because of the unusually frigid temperatures that year, his ears had been frostbitten repeatedly; they were swollen and peeling. He couldn't come up with a head-covering thick enough to protect his ears during the six hours a day he was standing up in the sled driving the team. Finally, the only recourse left seemed to be for Barney and Fran and I to move into the schoolhouse until the March blizzards were over. One brilliantly cold Sunday afternoon my father loaded some double-bed springs and a mattress into the box sled while we packed our suitcases and my mother assembled enough food to see us through from Monday to Friday. Then Nancy and Queen once more took us to the schoolhouse.

Dusk was coming on when my father turned the horses around to go home. With my face pressed against the small cloakroom window I watched the sled until it disappeared over the first hill. I then had a moment of panic, as if we had been marooned on a snow-covered island in the middle of a frozen ocean.

Barney hurriedly lit the kerosene lantern we had brought. This made matters worse. The schoolroom, which in the daytime had seemed small and contained, suddenly became a cavernous room with a high ceiling from which murky shadows poured down into every corner. As darkness came on, the blackboards covering three of the walls receded more and more into infinity, giving us the uneasy impression that we were living in a pavilion glassed in on one side and open on the others. When the room became chilly and Barney said she would have to go to the basement to stoke the furnace, we realized for the first time that we only had one lantern; all three of us went to the basement.

My mother had sent bread and butter, cornflakes, milk, peanut butter, apples, and roast beef. We ate our supper and then carefully rationed out some of the water from the two gallons we had brought for both drinking and washing. We went to bed early because there was nothing else to do. The lantern served only to spook us; it didn't give off enough light either to do homework or correct papers.

We had no more than settled in bed, however, before a strong northwest wind blew up and began to rattle the six west windows. As the wind intensified the rafters began to creak; with each fresh blast of wind the entire structure shuddered. I was certain it was going to collapse on our heads, and I burrowed deep under the covers between Barney and Fran and put my hands over my ears. They assured me that in all of their long lives they had never heard of a schoolhouse blowing down, that schoolhouses were not made to blow down. Fran put it to me straight. "You're ten years old and in all of that time did you ever hear of a schoolhouse blowing down?" I had to admit I hadn't, so I went to sleep.

I awoke in the middle of the night to find Barney and Fran sitting up in bed looking ghostly. The wind had died down, but now in the sudden quiet there was a new insidious noise. Something powerful was shoving against the south side of the schoolhouse wall, as if it were trying to push over the building. We huddled together in bed, not daring to move. Just when we began to think that whoever or whatever it was had left, there would be another ominous shove and a low grinding crunch in the snow. When dawn began to light up the windows, we heard a telltale nicker. We threw the bedcovers off and ran to the windows in time to see a band of small white mustangs streaking across the prairie; they had spent the night against the schoolhouse wall to shelter themselves against the wind.

The next night they returned. Fran bundled up and went around the corner of the schoolhouse armed with a broom to frighten them away. They galloped off, but Fran had no more than removed her galoshes before they were back, stamping and shoving for position. They had obviously staked their claim to the schoolhouse wall long before we arrived, and they were not going to let any Johnnies-come-lately jump it. They always left as the first streaks of daylight began to appear, running into the dawn and nickering for each other as if they had definite business elsewhere.

We had expected to go home every weekend, but we only made it home once in the next five weeks. Every time Friday rolled around another blizzard moved in, and my father was afraid that if he took us home he wouldn't be able to get us back by Monday morning. Barney felt a tremendous responsibility to be in school on time each morning, because most of her pupils lived close enough to walk to school; when they reached it they needed immediate shelter and warmth. My father came in to see us several times a week, bringing food and fresh clothing and the back issues of the *Minneapolis Journal* so we could keep up on the comic strips.

What Barney and I had going for us that long winter in the schoolhouse was Fran, who was twelve going on thirty. She had just the kind of bravado that was needed in our situation. When the mustangs became so rambunctious in the early morning hours that Barney and I were certain the wall was going to cave in, Fran awoke only to remark that this sort of thing didn't bother her at all. And when the blizzards shook the rafters in forty-mile-an-hour winds she brought out the deck of cards and in the dim light of the swaying lantern soundly rousted me in a few games of gin rummy. This made me so angry that I forgot about everything except my rabid conviction that she was cheating and I couldn't catch her at it. Although Fran proclaimed time and again that there was nothing to be afraid of, that we were, in fact, having an easy time of it ("See, we don't even have to get up and go to school. Here we are"), Barney and I did discover a tiny chink in her armor. One morning when she was dressing she noticed a strange lump in the hem of her corduroy skirt. She ripped open the seam and found a dead mouse. She turned pale and looked spooked the rest of the day.

As I looked out of the cloakroom window on a Friday afternoon the second week in April and saw my father charging through the melting snow in his truck to move us home, I thought I had never seen a more beautiful sight. When I walked into the house I thought I would never again see one so luxurious. I became instantly aware of relativity: relative to the schoolhouse, our farmhouse was a mansion. My mother had entertained her Ladies Aid that afternoon, and the house was spruced up to a turn. She had made her famous tangy potato salad and her special three-day fat brown buns that were so light they floated through the ceiling. There was molded strawberry Jell-O with chopped apples. I thought I would never stop eating. That evening I sat on my mother's lap in front of the coal range in the kitchen, and I promised myself that I would never leave home again.

The next winter, nevertheless, when the March blizzards again swept down from Canada on a prairie that was inert under immovable expanses of impacted snow, Barney and I once more were encamped in the schoolhouse. But this time it was a whole new ballgame because we didn't have Fran; she had moved on to high school. Without her, Barney and I rattled around in the murky schoolhouse at night like two nervous pebbles in a drum. Instead of closing my eyes when I went to bed I'd follow the shadows creeping down around the corners of all those blackboards, and then my teeth would start chattering. If I hadn't fallen asleep before the mustangs arrived, there was no hope for me; I'd begin to shake for fair, and Barney would have to sit up with me for the remainder of the night.

The two of us stood it for just one week. After my father had brought us home for the weekend, I heard Barney tell my mother when she thought I was asleep that there was no way in the world she was going to spend another night in that Godforsaken schoolhouse with a quivering child— teaching or no teaching. So my father spent not only the rest of the winter, but much of the following one as well, taking Barney and me back and forth to school in the box sled with Nancy and Queen. Each year Queen became lazier and more recalcitrant. My father was perpetually hoarse from shouting, "QVEEN!"

I heard my father say many times after it was all over that he wouldn't go through those three years again that Barney taught Freeman School Number One if someone handed him *ti tusen dollar.* Ten thousand dollars. It was the most ridiculous sum anyone could think of after a half-dozen years in the Dust Bowl.

Barney's salary during her three years of teaching country school was sixty dollars a month, but the township

*The Education of a Family*                    35

didn't have the money to pay her because scarcely any of the farmers could pay their taxes. Instead of giving her a negotiable check, the township gave her a "warrant," which was a cash-it-when-you-can promissory note to pay whenever funds became available. Because Barney was sending Florence to the University of North Dakota she was desperate to collect her salary, and—like most of the other country schoolteachers in North Dakota during the Dust Bowl—she searched around for someone who would cash her warrants for a discount. Many agencies dealing in "warrant cashing" sprang up during this period. Although they were usurious, they were also high-risk enterprises that served a purpose; they probably earned the high rates they charged. Barney found an agency in Bismarck that cashed her warrants for a 15 percent discount. She received fifty-one dollars in cash through the mail and counted herself lucky. It was enough to get Florence through two years at the university and a Bachelor of Arts in education.

Florence was still only nineteen years old, but she was finally old enough to teach. She said that all her life she had waited for her age to catch up to the station she had already reached. She found a job teaching high school English in a tiny town in eastern North Dakota called Doyon. Her salary was a munificent seventy-five dollars a month, and the school district was solvent; she didn't have to take a warrant. She immediately began to send Norman to the University of North Dakota.

Barney was able to save all of her discounted warrant money during her third year of teaching, so the following year she went off to the University of North Dakota herself to work toward her degree. That same year I joined Gladys and Fran in Williston High School. We had a small efficiency apartment. My mother every week brought us homemade bread, butter, meat, and a cake. Gladys and Fran were much in demand as babysitters; they earned twenty-five to fifty cents several nights a week. I was only thirteen and small for my age so I didn't get any baby-sitting jobs but, on the other hand, my size stood me in good stead. When we went to the movies, which was our only recreation, I got in for a child's ticket at fifteen cents instead of a student's at twenty-five cents. My sisters, who always chipped in for my ticket, admonished me not to grow another inch until I could pay my own way.

During my initial year in high school I was constantly in a turmoil about one thing or another. Homesickness plagued me like a nagging toothache, and I couldn't sleep because the street traffic kept me awake. It was almost worse than the mustangs. When I heard the delivery trucks roaring on the other side of my window all of my reflexes told me to leap up and run for cover.

Five hundred students shifted from classroom to class-room in the school's halls, and the year was half over before I had the lay of the land. Over a hundred students sat in study hall at once, presided over by a grim-faced, rigid-backed woman named Miss Moe, who had a British accent and patrolled the aisles constantly. She might as well have had two carbines strapped to her for the fear she instilled in me. Algebra was almost my downfall. When Fran, who was a whiz at anything mathematical (including gin rummy), finally realized I was going under, she grabbed me and tutored me every night until she had me treading water. No sister of *hers* was going to flunk anything as elementary as algebra.

It was now 1937, and the prairies after eight years of drought were so parched that for two or three years many of the farmers had not found it worthwhile to have their crops threshed. My father, however, in 1934 had purchased a small combine in partnership with my mother's brother who lived across the road. Each remaining year of the thirties they pulled the combine over their wheat fields and managed to glean two or three bushels to the acre—counting the hollows—enough to pay their real estate taxes.

Other than that, we lived solely from the cows and the chickens. My parents milked a dozen cows, separated the milk in their DeLaval cream separator, and sold the cream to the Farmers Union Cooperative Creamery in Williston. My mother's cream checks purchased shoes and the fabrics with which she made all of our clothes and contributed to the child in college who needed it most. The chickens kept us in groceries. Every week my mother took anywhere from three to twelve dozen (in the summer) eggs to a Williston grocery and traded them for sugar, flour, coffee, and a few canned vegetables. She never bought more than the eggs traded for. If she needed anything more, she waited until the next week. She didn't need much. My father butchered hogs and steers and had the meat packaged and stored in a frozen-food locker in town. My mother churned her own butter, rendered her own lard, made her own bread, and canned whatever she could glean out of the summer's parched garden. She always had rhubarb, with which she filled her canning shelves each year, and which we despised. And, of course, potatoes. There was never a year so dry that a potato would not grow—would not insist on growing—in the North Dakota soil. My father always planted an acre of potatoes. He dug them up in the fall and stored them directly on the earth in the root cellar. There were always enough left for seed the following spring.

When Barney came home from the University of North Dakota at the end of the year, she was distraught because for the first time in her life she had flunked a course. She said it was because she couldn't see; that, in fact, she could see nothing out of one eye. My father took her to a Williston optometrist who agreed she couldn't see, but he didn't know the reason. My father then took her to Minot, where a new eye clinic had already gained a fine reputation for its advanced techniques. The doctors there said she had a detached retina. She stayed at the clinic for three months, during which she remained in bed with her eyes bandaged. She was given daily sweat baths, the theory being that extreme dehydration would eventually draw the retina back in place. When this didn't work, the doctors performed surgery and sewed the retina back. It was the first surgery of its kind at the clinic and one of the first in the country and was written up in a medical journal. The surgery was termed successful in that it saved her physical eye, but the vision was gone.

Barney went home to convalesce for the rest of the winter. She had an enormous hospital bill which she was unable to pay. The doctors at the clinic had been incredibly nice about it—had, in fact, never asked her how or when she was going to pay her bill. The day she left, she had told them that if they would be patient and wait until she had finished college, she could then get a job teaching high school with a salary large enough that she could begin to pay off her bill.

The doctors said they thought that was a splendid idea.

Barney returned to the University of North Dakota for the summer session. To earn her expenses, she worked as a live-in nursemaid for the children of a Grand Forks doctor and tutored English on the side. She received her degree the following June, and in the fall she secured a job teaching high school English at Hague, a small town on the border of North and South Dakota. With her first paycheck she began to pay off her hospital bill. The next year she moved on to a higher-paying job teaching English in Pierce, Idaho, and the year after she bettered herself again in the larger nearby city of Lewiston. It had taken a big portion of her salary for three years, but in the spring of 1942 she was finally out of debt.

In the interim years, the rest of us continued our stepping-stone efforts to complete our educations. By the time I was a junior in Williston High School, both Gladys and Fran were attending college in Minot. Gladys had left Minot State Teachers College after a year and had enrolled in the city business college. To pay her expenses she clerked in a small family grocery. She lived in a room above the market. One night the building caught fire and she was rescued from the second-story window by a city fireman, who carried her down the ladder in her nightgown. Although the smoke had hurt her lungs and she coughed for months afterward, she had a wonderful time recounting the incident. Every time she told the story, the fireman who rescued her became younger and handsomer and her nightgown scantier—until I began to envy her for having had the rare good fortune of such a romantic experience. She continued to work in the grocery until she graduated from business college and became a stenographer.

Fran, the whiz kid, attended Minot State Teachers College continuously, summer and winter, working in the library to earn most of her expenses and graduating in three years. She secured a job teaching high school mathematics and science in a crossroads town called Bowdon in central North Dakota. With her first paycheck she bought me a beautiful red wool dress trimmed in green velvet. It was the first dress I owned that my mother hadn't made for me.

At the end of his third year at the University of North Dakota, Norman decided that Florence must be freed of the responsibility for any more of his education, although he had helped defray his college costs with part-time jobs. Only a year apart in age, he and Florence were like twins in their devotion to each other. She begged him to finish out his last year, reminding him that from the time they were children they had always been partners. Together they had herded cattle, stacked clover hay, shocked wheat, and driven farm machinery; now she wanted to see him through to his college graduation. But Norman was adamant. With his three years of training in mechanical engineering, he was able to get a job as a surveyor with a road builder.

I was one of the lucky ones. The year I started college the rains began to come back to the prairies and my parents' financial situation eased. The 1941 wheat harvest was the first decent crop my parents had had in eleven years. My father was so buoyant it was as if a decade had been lifted from his walk. He went to the courthouse and paid seven years of back personal property taxes, on which the state had declared a moratorium. The receipts from that day, jauntily rolled up with a rubber band, were still in his safety deposit box after his death twenty-two years later.

Shortly before noon on December 8, 1941, I sat on the floor in the lounge of Dakota Hall at Minot State Teachers College with a hundred other young women and listened to President Roosevelt's announcement of Pearl Harbor. When we returned to our classes that afternoon, there were no boys. They were all out enlisting.

War can change a family's pattern more rapidly than anything, and ours was no exception. Before another two years were out, all five of us sisters were in the Twin Cities. And Norman was a fighter pilot with the Twin Dragon 459th Fighter Squadron, flying P-38s over Burma.

Florence had married and was living with her baby in St. Paul while her husband was in the marines. She and her baby shared their apartment with Gladys and Fran. Gladys was in the stenographic pool at the Ford Motor plant, where armored cars were made, and Fran worked as a chemist in a laboratory at Minneapolis Honeywell, which had also converted to the war effort. Barney was teaching high school English in a Minneapolis suburb. I had transferred to the University of Minnesota to be close to my sisters. I was majoring in journalism and working as a reporter on the *Minnesota Daily*; it was shorthanded because of the war. I was paid ten cents per column inch of published copy, measured by yardstick. One historic month I wrote an even four yards and made $14.40. I could never top it.

Every weekend we five sisters converged in Florence's apartment and sat around the playpen in the living room, drinking the tea to which we were trying to become accustomed, coffee being rationed. Florence's baby had five mothers for the first two years of her life.

My graduation from the University of Minnesota in June 1944 was the culmination of my mother's struggle to educate her children.

For her oldest daughter, though, the struggle was not quite over. Barney decided that she was tired of teaching —weary of those desolate towns in which she had taught all over North Dakota, Idaho, and Minnesota. What she had secretly wanted to be all her life, Barney said, was a nurse.

She applied for admission to the U.S. Cadet Nurse Corps. Because she was thirty years old and had vision in only one eye, she held out little hope for acceptance. But the government was very anxious, not knowing how long the war would go on, to build up a reserve of nurses; Barney was promptly inducted after agreeing to be available "for military or other essential civilian services for the duration of the war." She subsequently went through a grueling two and a half years of accelerated training at the University of Minnesota School of Nursing and declared she loved every day of it. She said that she felt her entire life had been vindicated when she graduated at the top of her class. She had hoped to serve overseas, but the war was over.

Released from her obligations to the U.S. Cadet Nurse Corps, Barney was free to go anywhere she wanted, and she was besieged with job offers. The shortage of nurses was still acute. Especially in demand were older women who held both Graduate in Nursing and bachelor's degrees and were capable of filling administrative positions. Barney accepted a job with the Department of Health in Mankato, a county-seat city in southern Minnesota. She had worked only a few months in her new career when one night she went on a blind date with a Minnesota farmer, fell in love with him, married him, and in nothing flat was a full-time farm wife.

It always gave my mother pause when she visited Barney on the farm after her marriage and observed her hoeing the garden, hauling grain to market, culling chickens, candling eggs, and sticking hypodermic needles into pigs and sheep. My mother would arrive home bemused. *Seven*

*years of college,* she would say, and if you wanted to count all of those summer sessions Barney had to attend to retain her teaching status, it would be more like *nine.* My mother would hasten to add that she had nothing against farmers, farmers were the best; it was just that Barney had struggled longer and harder for her education than any of her other children, and now she could have reaped the rewards of the *independence* she had earned to make her life *easier,* instead of taking on the kind of hard work that she herself had always had . . . and then my mother's voice would trail off.

My mother died before she knew how her thirteen grandchildren turned out, before she could know how they took to higher education like ducks to water. She would love to have toted up all of their advanced degrees, and if she could have watched their progress as they espoused one recondite profession after another, she would have been very proud. But she would not have been surprised, because she knew all along that with enough education anything is possible.

One of the last letters I received from my mother while she was still living on the farm fairly crackled with conflicting emotions as she recounted how a disgruntled high school student in the nearby town of Zahl had just burned down the school. At first she bristled with outrage at the mindlessness of a youth who could put a match to a temple of learning, but as her anger spent itself on the page the real tragedy of the situation began to engulf her.

"I don't suppose," she concluded sadly, "he will be going to school anymore now."

# 2

# The Seedling Years

*Did homestead wives on the western prairies learn* of necessity to cope with hard situations, or were they born to it? As they probably would have said themselves if they had been asked, "It was six one way, and half a dozen the other."

Whatever the reason, most of these women had an inner strength that seldom failed them. They could cry like babies at christenings and weddings, sniffling into their hemstitched handkerchiefs, but when the chips were down they were dry-eyed and fearless as lions. They could seize a garden hoe and cut a snake to ribbons who was approaching a baby on the grass. They could stand beside their husbands and beat off prairie fires with wet rugs. They could climb a seventy-foot windmill tower to bring down a terrified child. They could lance infected wounds. They didn't know what taking a vacation was.

Many of the women who came out to Williams County where my mother homesteaded were daughters of Norwegian immigrants who had settled in eastern North Dakota or other states a generation earlier. Some of them, like my mother, came alone to stake out homesteads for themselves; but the majority came after their husbands or fiancés had scouted the territory, staked a claim, and put up a cabin. Homesteading men were desperate for wives. After a man had managed to erect a twelve-by-twelve-foot tarpaper shanty or sod hut and had sat in it a month or two looking out at miles and miles of nothing but waving prairie grass or drifts of snow, he would go back to civilization for a few days and do almost anything to attract a woman adventurous enough and brave enough to follow him out to the frontier. The women who didn't want to be adventurous or brave shook their heads and stayed back home bending over their embroidery hoops or working as maids or seamstresses and eventually marrying someone with a safe job.

The women like my mother, who sought out the frontier on their own, knew exactly what they were getting into and were prepared to handle almost anything that came along; but the women who followed their husbands out must have received a shock from which it was difficult to recover. Having alighted from the train at the nearest railroad station with three or four trunks containing all of their worldly goods, they would be taken by horse and buggy or sled twenty or thirty miles out on the prairie and deposited in front of a homestead shack no bigger than the walk-in pantry back home. Where was the water? Down at the creek, miles away. Where was the outhouse? There was none. By this time, fortunately for their husbands, there was nothing for them to do but stay.

Having already lived in her own tiny homestead shack, which was just a hastily thrown-up tarpaper shanty so small she could barely turn around in it, my mother found my father's homestead cabin rather deluxe when she moved into it after their marriage. Compared to most of the other original dwellings on the prairies, it was an architectural beauty. About twelve by twenty-four feet long, it had a gabled, shingled roof with generous eaves, a sturdy brick chimney, and smooth horizontal clapboard siding. Wonder of wonders, it had a double-hung glass window at either end. My mother couldn't wait to start fixing it up.

The first major purchase she and my father made after their marriage was a Singer treadle sewing machine—a cabinet model into which the machine could be folded

*Carrine Gafkjen and Sever Berg, married very romantically on New Year's Eve, 1912, after having met at threshing time the previous summer. From the author's collection.*

down and the cover closed to double as a table. Although threshing machines and barbed wire are often given credit for settling the West, sewing machines could give them a run for their money. My mother always said that any homesteader's wife who didn't own a sewing machine might just as well have packed her trunks and headed back to her embroidery hoops, because there was no hope for her on the prairies.

Never able to tolerate a curtainless room, my mother first of all made ruffled cottage curtains for those amazing windows. She purchased fabric by the bolt. She made sheets, pillowcases, blankets, dish towels, tablecloths, and shirts for her husband. One thing she never did was baste. Any woman who couldn't sew a straight seam without basting, my mother said, had no business homesteading. She could make a pillowcase in five minutes. She'd take a square piece of cloth, put a three-inch hem on one side, fold the cloth in half, sew it up on three sides, turn it inside out, and behold, a pillowcase.

In those first months of her marriage my mother wallpapered the entire cabin, ceiling and all, with a strawberry print she ordered from Sears, Roebuck. It came complete with fake strawberries that hung several inches down from the ceiling. (How my father—the original no-frills man— must have loved that!)

In the spring of 1914, having lived on my father's homestead for a year and now expecting their first child, my parents decided to move the cabin to my mother's land, where they would build up their farm. It was not an easy decision for my father to make. He had earned the patent to his homestead the hard way—by living on the land continuously for five years. He had expected to live there the rest of his life, surrounded by and growing old with the other hardy young men of Norwegian descent who had staked claims to their homesteads at the same time and whom he had come to love. After having attempted for one year, however, to farm his own quarter of land in addition to hauling his farm equipment six miles into the next township to plant and harvest the crops on my mother's two quarters, he saw the wisdom of the move.

My mother had estimated that the baby was due the last week in May. My father and she planned to take the train to Minnesota two weeks before the birth to go to her parent's home where her mother—an experienced midwife— would deliver the baby.

On April 20 my father, with the help of both his old and new neighbors, moved his cabin on a horse-drawn flatbed to my mother's land. My mother had to pack up her household goods and put them in the lumber wagon for the trip. All that day she climbed up and down from the wagon dozens of times, transferring her belongings from cabin to wagon, and then back again from wagon to cabin at the new location. It never occurred to her, she said later,

*Nothing to Do but Stay*

that a thirty-five-year-old, eight-months pregnant woman shouldn't be jumping up and down from a lumber wagon.

That night she began to have labor pains. There wasn't a doctor or a midwife within twenty-five miles. My father put her in the wagon and took her a mile down the road to her cousin Tomas's homestead. She and Tomas, who grew up in Minnesota together as children, had met again in North Dakota and settled on adjoining pieces of land. His wife, Ingeborg, had never attended a birth before, but— strong woman that she was—she prided herself on never having failed at anything she set out to do, and she confidently delivered the baby girl.

My father must have been the only flustered one of the lot. When he went to the Williams County courthouse to fill out the birth certificate two days later, he not only misspelled his daughter's given names but missed his wife's age by one year and listed her birthplace in the wrong country.

It has always been incredible to me how fast my parents built up their farm, by their own sweat and paying for everything in cash from crops that were good one year and bad the next. By the time I, their sixth child, came along nine years later, they had established a farmstead that included a one-and-a-half-storied house, a barn, a 375-foot drilled well with a windmill, a two-storied granary, a chicken house, a hog pen, a blacksmith shop, a garage, two windbreak groves of cottonwood trees, and miles of barbed-wire fence. Their farm equipment included three teams of draft horses, a plow, drill, harrow, mower, rake, binder, two hay wagons, a lumber wagon, a box sled, a cream separator, and a Model T touring car. They milked a dozen cows, fed out a dozen steers and hogs, and kept two hundred chickens.

Much of those nine years my mother was pregnant. When I was born she was forty-four years old and by all odds—having borne five other children while building her share of the farmstead—she should have been worn out. Hardly. When I was six weeks old she brought me to church to be baptized in a long white gown, the lace of which she had found the time to crochet herself; her other children were starched to the teeth, and after church she brought the minister and half the congregation home for Sunday dinner.

I asked my mother once whether she really wanted me after having five other children. She replied that the only sadness she felt when I was born was that she knew I might be her last child. She told me then that some of the happiest moments of her life were in the first hours after a child was born, when she was lying in bed with the baby trying to nurse at her breast and the midwife in the kitchen making her a cup of coffee and a substantial meal. She said she was always so ravenously hungry she could scarcely resist getting out of bed and speeding up the process in the kitchen.

◆

Five daughters growing up who loved pretty clothes meant that my mother never stopped sewing. The treadle machine sat in the kitchen in front of the south window, most of the time with a garment in progress. My mother was not only a fast seamstress, she was an ingenious one. In the early years before commercial patterns became readily available, she made her own. From an old newspaper she could cut out a dress pattern in half an hour, complete with Peter Pan collars, peplums, puffed sleeves, gored skirts, gussets, or any other detail that might strike our fancy. She'd put the extra leaf in the kitchen table, spread out the fabric, pin on the pattern, cut it out, sit down at her treadle machine, and by nightfall one of us would have a new dress. If she made a coat or a two-piece suit, it might take her two or three days. The last garment my mother ever made for me—when I left home for my first job after graduating from college—was a coral linen suit lined in gold silk; I wore it for two decades afterward.

Quilting was another of my mother's never-ending projects. An enormous number of quilts were needed to keep a family of eight warm at night through the long and harsh North Dakota winters. The loft in which we children slept was not only uninsulated but unheated, except for a twelve-inch square cut into the floor which allowed a small amount of warm air to come through from the parlor beneath. By morning we could always see our breath. We five sisters slept in two double beds, and Norman had a cot in a corner under the eaves. I had the warmest spot in the loft, in the center of a double bed between Gladys and Fran. We had so many quilts over us—usually five—that it took all three of us to lift them enough to turn in bed. When we wanted to turn over, one of us would say, "Turn!"

There was only one set of quilting frames in the neighborhood, and they belonged to Ingeborg. The story of how she acquired them was one of the most delicious tales in the community. When Ingeborg and Tomas first moved out to their homestead cabin, Ingeborg was appalled when she realized she had no quilting frames, nor did any of the other wives nearby. She started to nag her husband, who was an expert carpenter, into making her some frames, but he was busy with a thousand and one jobs he considered more important, and he never got to it. She kept nagging and nagging to no avail. This went on until Tomas decided he was going to build a new house, and he subsequently made his first trip to Williston with the lumber wagon and a team of horses to bring home a stack of new lumber. It was a fifty-mile round trip, and it took him two days. He started early in the morning, reached Williston after dark, stayed overnight, got up before dawn and

*Nothing to Do but Stay*

loaded up his lumber, and didn't get home until almost midnight. The next week he made a second trip. When he returned home, thirty-six hours later, he found that his wife had a new set of quilting frames. In his absence she had helped herself to a couple of the two-by-fours he had purchased on his first trip. She had cut them into four lengths with his carpenter's saw, after which she had taken up his brace and bit and drilled holes every three inches through the boards. She had then ransacked his toolbox and had found four long iron bolts with which to fit the frames together at the corners. Ingeborg was not handy with an auger, and boring the holes had taken her many hours and left her hands red with splinters, but she finally had her quilting frames!

My mother and every other wife in the neighborhood borrowed those frames dozens of times over the years, and every time they stretched the quilts on the boards they laughed and remembered Ingeborg's wrath as she drilled and drilled in her husband's absence.

Two days of my mother's week were consumed in doing the laundry for her family of eight. My mother thought she had to boil everything white. Before dawn on Monday morning she brought in the giant oblong washboiler and set it on the stove, filling it with four or five pails of soft water pumped from the cistern. She added soap and put in the bed linens, handkerchiefs, tablecloths, underwear, and white shirts. She brought the whole mess to a boil and kept on boiling and boiling for at least a half an hour, stirring with a long stick. She transferred the clothes with the stick to a washtub, which she had set up on two kitchen chairs pushed together. Rubbing the clothes vigorously up and down on the scrubboard, she was soon wet with perspiration. After wringing the clothes out and putting them through two rinses, one of blueing water, she was finally ready to put them out on the clothesline.

My mother was never fussier about anything than hanging clothes on the line. Anyone driving down the road, she said, could see your entire life hanging on the line for judgment, and a carelessly hung wash was the sure sign of a *sjusket kvinne*—a slattern. Each garment had to be attached to its neighbor by a common clothespin, and they could not be *slack*. They must all hang *taut*. All of the colored clothes, even the men's socks, had to be turned inside out so they wouldn't fade. Even in the coldest part of the winter, my mother always hung out the wash, although it froze solid in a few minutes. She held the opinion that the cold air freshened the clothes and got out at least some of the water. The frozen clothes had to be brought indoors again and hung on wooden clothes-racks to dry around the stove.

My mother spent every Monday from dawn until late afternoon doing the family wash. It was probably no acci-

*Nothing to Do but Stay*

dent that four out of six of her children were born on Tuesday.

If she wasn't having a baby on Tuesday, my mother ironed. She had three flatirons, which she heated on top of her kitchen range and which she lifted with a detachable handle. She changed irons about every ten minutes as they cooled off. When I awakened on Tuesday morning, I could hear my mother ironing. The handle squeaked as it was pushed against the flatiron moving across the ironing board. One Christmas my father bought her an outsized gasoline iron, which was equipped with a small gas tank on the back; it had to be generated like a gas lamp before being lit. My mother loved that iron. It had such a large smooth surface, and she didn't have to heat up the coal range as she did with her old flatirons. But all day the carbon monoxide fumes drifted up in her face, and by the end of the day she had a splitting headache. Still, she refused to give it up; she thought the headaches were worth the time it saved. One Tuesday, however, she was in a hurry, and she didn't generate the iron long enough. It started to puff, and she hurled it out the kitchen door a second before it burst into flames. It couldn't have happened to a nicer piece of equipment.

Feeding the minister was one of the preoccupations of pioneer women. It was not as simple as it sounds. It was, in fact, a delicate procedure requiring diplomacy and exquisite timing. My mother and the other homesteaders' wives in the congregation spent a lot of time at it.

Standing on a slight rise a mile down the road from our farm, the church was an austerely beautiful wood structure with a white steeple housing the great bell whose peal could be heard on Sunday morning rolling over the prairies for miles in every direction. Built by the homesteaders, who had hauled the lumber with wagons and horses twenty-eight miles from Williston, it was either a large church or a small church, depending on what age you were when you last saw it. When I was a child I considered it frighteningly cavernous, the cathedral ceiling so high I was certain it was the floor of heaven. When thirty years later I returned to visit it I couldn't believe how the church had shrunk.

Because there were only a dozen families in the community, the congregation couldn't afford its own exclusive pastor; it was necessary to share him with three other rural congregations in contiguous townships. The pastor lived in the parsonage in Zahl, a small town about ten miles away from the closest church. Each of his parishes was at least ten miles apart. If he drove like a madman he could get in four sermons every Sunday. After his first service at ten A.M., a family in this congregation would invite him out to the farm for a noon dinner. He would have very little time to dally over his meal because he had another ten-mile drive to reach his next parish by one o'clock. After this service was completed, he had time only to shake a few hands as he walked down the aisle before he must leap into his automobile to career across the prairies ten or fifteen miles to his third parish for the four P.M. service. A farm family here would invite him home for supper, and after that—logged with food and no time to digest it—he would drive to his last service at eight in the evening.

The services were staggered; we went to church at a different time every Sunday. When our service was in the morning, one of the twelve matrons in our parish had to ask the minister home for dinner. When it occurred at four o'clock in the afternoon, my mother or one of her neighbors had to ask him for supper.

The first order of business at the Ladies Aid, which met once a month at the farm home of one of the members, was to work out the schedule for the following month. The president of the Aid would get out her work sheet.

"It says here we will be having the ten o'clock service on the fifteenth. Now who will take the preacher?"

Much buzzing back and forth. Taking the preacher is not a decision to be made without forethought.

"I could take him but I got relatives coming."

"I could take him if my boys get over the chicken pox. Do you think the reverend has had the pox?"

"You better wait your turn until next month, Helga."

Gunilla finally decides she can take him. Then they go through it all over again for the four o'clock service. "Now who can take the preacher on the twenty-ninth?"

The matron who had elected to feed him on any particular Sunday had to stay home that day to cook, because there was no letting the minister cool his heels in the parlor; even a half hour's wait could ruin his day's schedule. So it was up to the husband to go to church and invite the pastor home for dinner. On occasion, when the husband wasn't quick enough about stepping out into the aisle to intercept him, another husband (whose wife had been absent from the Aid the previous month and had taken it into her head all on her own to take the preacher) would invite him. The first husband's life wasn't worth much when he came home that day, nor were negotiations peaceful at the next meeting of the Ladies Aid.

For the minister, of course, every matron threw out all of her cooking stops. By the time she had a Sunday meal on the table for him, this was as fancy as she was going to get. She had broken out her finest linen tablecloth and napkins, starched within an inch of their lives, and the table was laden from end to end with all the delicacies her garden, her pantry, and her considerable expertise could produce. It held her best preserves, mashed potatoes and gravy, two kinds of meat (*always* two kinds of meat), vegetables, homemade bread, not to mention a pie cooling in the kitchen. But when the time actually came when she

*Nothing to Do but Stay*

would usher the minister in from the parlor and ask him to sit up to the table, she would pull out his chair, wring her hands, and say apologetically, "Now you will just have to try and make a meal out of this, Reverend!"

For several decades this same sentence was accepted silently by every minister who served the territory—and there were many of them because their average tenure was from three to five years. But one year a new minister came—a stern fire-and-brimstone man who was a veteran of many a missionary outpost and who brooked no non-sense; he was as bristly as the red mustache on his upper lip. And even he endured the sentence for many months of Sundays.

And then he must have said to himself, "Enough is enough." Because one Sunday he preached a fiery sermon on hypocrisy, invoking both the Old Testament and the New, pounding his fist on the pulpit, pointing a stern finger to heaven and then to hell, and shouting with such rage that the rafters shook. Then his voice dropped to a whisper. "And what about the good ladies of my parish? Their tables groan from the weight of enough food to feed a multitude, and they say, 'Now you must try to make a meal of this, Reverend!'"

For reasons that were never made clear in the minutes of the church council meeting, this particular pastor didn't last even the obligatory three years. He soon moved on to another territory—where perhaps the cooks were spartan and without guile.

◈

No matter how busy the pioneer women were with their own tasks, when their husbands came to them and said they were needed, they dropped everything and went. From the time she was married my mother always helped my father outside. The first year she helped him clear the rocks from his homestead quarter and both of her own—a bone-crushing job. My father dug out the largest rocks from the soil with a pickax, and my mother helped him carry or roll them onto a flat stoneboat pulled by a team of horses. Today, seventy-five years later, the huge rock piles still lie in the corners of their quarter sections—indestructible evidence of their earliest labors.

Even in later years if my brother wasn't home and my father couldn't get a hired man my mother would often go out into the fields and help my father rake hay or operate the binder that tied the wheat into sheaves. She always helped my father milk cows, morning and evening, summer and winter, no matter how busy she was in the house. There seemed to be an unspoken understanding between them that this was a job they must share.

During the course of my childhood I realized more and more that my parents had many unspoken understandings of which I only occasionally saw a glimmer. One of them

*Nothing to Do but Stay*

was that they never called each other by name. I can never remember my mother and father calling each other anything at all. When they spoke they just looked into each other's eyes and started talking. When my mother spoke to someone else about my father she used his name. When my father mentioned my mother in conversation he would say "she" or *"kjerring,"* wife. When I became aware of this strange custom I began to observe how the other homesteaders addressed their spouses, and I soon discovered they didn't call each other anything either.

Was it because they were so neutral about each other? On the contrary, I think it was the other way around: they had been through so much together and their feelings ran so deeply for each other that they couldn't bear to utter anything as intimate as their spouses' names in front of anyone—not even their children.

My mother and the other original pioneer women who lived to be a great age achieved what amounted to almost sainthood in their communities in their last years. There would never be others to take their place. There was no need. The land was settled. The backbreaking work was done.

No one recognized this more than their daughters, who, even though they might still live on the old homesteads and still work hard, now had refrigerators and freezers, washers and dryers, and electric milking machines and sewing machines to lessen the load.

In their last years, my mother and the other pioneer women who were her neighbors were no longer called by their first names. Whereas in the early years they had been called Carrine and Ingeborg and Ericka and Gunilla and Hilda, they were now addressed as Mrs. Berg and Mrs. Quie and Mrs. Ryen and Mrs. Walstad and Mrs. Thorstad. The amusing thing is that they even stopped calling *each other* by their first names. It was as if they didn't want to be disrespectful to each other by breaking the pattern.

The holdouts were their husbands, who had never, of course, called them anything, and that's the way it remained until the end.

*Nothing to Do but Stay*

# 3

## Prairie Cook

*My mother was fond of saying that anyone could be a* fine cook if unlimited ingredients were available; to prepare tasty and attractive food with what one had on hand was the real challenge. If my gustative memories of childhood on the western plains serve me right—and they seem to become more salivary with the years—my mother and most of the other hardy young women of Norwegian descent who set up housekeeping in tiny homestead cabins in the early 1900s were more than up to the challenge.

When I think of the food of my childhood, I think first of holidays: of the *lutefisk* and *lefse,* of the delicately spicy Norwegian meatballs in gravy, of the nothing-but-butter cookies—the *sandbakkels,* the *spritz,* and the *berliner-kranzer.* I close my eyes and smell the breathtaking icy freshness of the hand-cranked ice cream on Christmas eve at the very moment the handle is taken off the freezer and the ice is cleared away and the cover is lifted from the steel container to reveal the heavenly frozen swirl beneath. Because I am the youngest child, I am given a teaspoon and allowed the heady first dip.

Then I think of harvesttime. I see the great threshing machine in a vast wheatfield of golden shocks of grain that stand out like miniature Indian tepees as far as the eye can sweep. I hear the curious drumbeat of the steam engine, see the high blower puffing out straw hour after hour until at dusk there is a perfect cone-shaped yellow stack looming up against the horizon. I see a dozen wagons piled high with sheaves lined up behind the threshing machine, the men perched up on the sheaves as they wait their turns to throw the bundles into the separator. Their teams of horses stand patiently, half asleep, lulled by the beat of the steam engine. The faces of the men are covered with wheat chaff, and their lips stand out crimson from the irritation of the dust.

A moment later I see my mother in the kitchen. She is lining a large dishpan with a snowy floursack dish towel and heaping it high with butter sandwiches and doughnuts. I see her standing over the black cast-iron range making coffee in a giant granite coffeepot, see her vigorously grinding the coffee at the hand grinder on the wall, see her mixing the ground coffee with an egg—shell and all—and dropping it into the pot, pouring boiling water over it, letting it settle, then pouring a cup of cream into it.

She lifts the coffeepot from the stove and walks out the door with it, trailed by my sisters Gladys and Fran carrying the dishpan between them and by my brother Norman carrying the tin pail full of cups. I tag along, barefoot, for the pure joy of it as they walk out to the threshing rig to serve the men their nine A.M. coffee break. Only we don't call it coffee break. We call it "forenoon lunch."

The men jump down from their wagons and squat on their haunches to form a circle around us. My mother pours the coffee into the thick white china cups and passes them around to the men. They wipe the chaff from their red lips with the back of their sleeves and take the first swallow of the coffee as strong and nut-brown as the prairie itself.

The men each take a sandwich or two, but they reach more eagerly for the doughnuts, because my mother is a superb doughnut maker, having made at least enough of them in her lifetime to provide her with a chain link to heaven. They are firm and rich and deeply browned, ideal for dunking, and they will stick to a man's ribs until dinnertime.

Like the captain of a ship who is the last to descend, the

owner of the threshing rig comes last for his coffee, after most of the men have gone back to their wagons. Having known each other from homestead days, he and my mother do a little joshing (no one ever kids on the prairies), and my mother laughs and her dark eyes flash, making her look suddenly young and pretty.

As we start back to the kitchen, my sisters and I reach for the remaining doughnuts in the dishpan. Even to us, they taste better out in the field. We make a similar trip at four P.M., and we call this "afternoon lunch." There are, of course, also breakfast, dinner, and supper—which the men eat in the kitchen. At the 4:30 A.M. breakfast there are soda pancakes and fried eggs in butter with salt pork on the side. At dinner there are mountains of mashed potatoes, fried beefsteak, creamed carrots and peas, pickled beets, bread and butter, and my mother's famous lemon meringue pie. At supper there are American fried potatoes, cold sliced roast pork, scalloped macaroni and tomatoes, dill pickles, and my mother's renowned devil's food cake with rhubarb sauce.

It is almost dark before the last man has left the kitchen after supper. My mother and my two older sisters, Barney and Florence, wash dishes until almost midnight. They run out of dry dish towels, so Gladys and Fran and I must stand outside and wave the wet ones dry. The dazzling North Dakota sky is peppered with stars from horizon to horizon, and I have a feeling of unrealness, because I am usually in bed at this hour. The mournful strains of a guitar waft up from the barn, where the threshing crew has bedded down in the hayloft for the night. A man named Bjerne has a crush on Florence, but he is too shy to tell her, except by song:

> From this valley they say you are going.
> When you go may your darling go, too.
> Would you leave him behind broken-hearted
> When he loves not another but you.

A few minutes later, having apparently given up hope and now in deep despair, Bjerne switches his tune:

> Write me a letter,
> Send it by mail,
> Send it in care of
> The Birmingham Jail.

We three little girls giggle, and as we hand the dish towels in to Florence, we notice that her cheeks are bright and hot.

The community threshing rigs I remember as a child in the thirties were considerably scaled down from the sprawling steam threshing rigs for which my mother cooked in the early 1900s after she had proved up her homestead. Then, because the land was still being settled, homesteads were often miles apart, and one rig served an area of twenty or thirty miles. Unlike the later community operations, when each farmwife cooked for the threshers as they came along, the early rigs were forced to equip and transport a cook car. Wages for cooks were sky-high, because all the men in the territory were needed for the threshing operation itself. There were scarcely any women in the area available or willing to take on the job: sleeping and traveling in a tin-covered boxcar the size of a haywagon, getting up at three in the morning to make pancakes for thirty or forty men, making quantities of bread in a makeshift oven, frying hundreds of doughnuts every day for morning and afternoon coffee breaks, making pies by the dozen.

But to my mother, who had spent years in Minneapolis cooking for a family of ten in addition to keeping a twenty-one-room, three-storied Victorian house in order, this was duck soup. Besides, the men in the threshing crew loved her. They couldn't believe her cooking. The first week in the season she cooked for them they grabbed entire pies and ate them singlehanded. My mother just smiled and pushed another pie at them. After two weeks she had them so stuffed they were taking one piece at a time. Just to keep them interested, she occasionally covered the potatoes with a fancy French sauce she had learned in her Minneapolis days.

Tending the coals for the threshing rig's steam engine

one summer was a man with the clearest, bluest eyes she had ever seen. Under their steady gaze her own dark eyes fell in confusion. He wasn't much of an eater. He picked at the tangy filling of her lemon meringue pie and had the audacity to leave on his plate the incredibly flaky crust that was the talk of four townships. Although born in North Dakota's Red River valley, he spoke Halling like a trooper. He courted my mother in a rented surrey on a rainy day when the steam engine stood idle. No word of English was spoken between them on that day—or ever after.

When I think of the food of my childhood, I never think of it as lacking in variety—a tribute to my mother's ingenuity. The two categories of food that were lacking on the prairies were fruits and vegetables. The growing season was much too short for fruit. Frost came too early in the fall and stayed too late in the spring. Oranges were rare items that appeared in our Christmas stockings. Apples were available only in the winter when they were shipped in from the West in bushel crates. And the only vegetable that would grow with certainty, year in and year out— even in the Dust Bowl years—were potatoes. In good years, carrots, peas, beets, onions, and cucumbers also grew well.

But the North Dakota soil seemed to be able to produce

potatoes under any conditions. When all else failed during the drought years, of which there were many, potatoes provided the homesteaders with an abundantly nutritious food—their only regular source of vitamin C. My mother often served potatoes twice a day. Far from tiring of them, I still love them so much that if I could choose one food to be marooned with on a desert island, I'd probably take potatoes. I'd take them boiled, baked, mashed, scalloped, or browned. But above all, I'd take them in my mother's potato salad.

One taste of my mother's potato salad and it was indelibly imprinted on your palate, leaving you forever immune to paler versions. To make the dressing, she put a dozen egg yolks in a saucepan, together with two cups of vinegar, two tablespoons of mustard, a tablespoon of salt, and a half cup of sugar. She cooked this mixture very slowly until it was thick, after which she beat in a couple of tablespoons of butter. After this had cooled, she added an equal amount, more or less, of thick sour cream, tasting and adding until she had the flavor just right. If she happened to have some new onions in the garden, she snipped off a few green tops, diced them, and added them. My mother's potato salad was so savory that there was seldom any left over on the second day, but if there was, it was so zingy that one dish of it would float you to the ceiling, where, suspended, you were quite willing to die happy.

*Nothing to Do but Stay*

We always had boiled potatoes the day before my mother made bread. Pioneer women quickly learned that bread made with potato water remained moist much longer than that made with milk or water alone. My mother's bread was gutsy but tender-crusted and full of flavor. She always set her yeast sponge the night before with the hard, cornmeal yeastcake she bought in two-inch squares at the country store. She made twelve loaves at a time, once a week, and baked them in three tremendous black bread pans that held four loaves each.

Her oven had a crack in it and didn't bake evenly, so she had to keep turning the pans and trading them off from the top shelf to the bottom shelf to get them all browned. Sometimes, if the wind was from the wrong direction and her stove didn't get a draft, she baked bread far into the evening. Earlier in the day, while stoking the range with enough wood and coal to get the oven hot enough to bake twelve loaves of bread at once, my mother baked her week's supply of cakes, pies, and cookies.

◈

Because life on the prairies was often harsh and filled with long, tedious days of nothing but sunup-to-sundown hard physical labor, holidays were eagerly looked forward to as a time of respite when neighbors and relatives could get together, swap hard-times stories, and do a little joshing in an atmosphere of good fellowship and good food. The

*A settlers' picnic my mother attended while still single. She is seated at center in the ruffled white dress and flared hat. Lounging at her right elbow is her cousin Tomas Quie, who homesteaded on an adjoining quarter. From the author's collection.*

women trotted out the fancy and often complicated recipes they had inherited from their mothers and grandmothers in Norway.

Far and away the most popular of these was *lefse*. Made from—what else—potatoes! To a Norwegian American, *lefse* epitomizes the spirit of the Old Country: it is visceral, hearty, chewy, filling, and altogether satisfying. For lack of a better word, it is often described as a potato pancake, and, indeed, *lefse* as it is made in this country today—in the modern electric *lefse* griddles—might correctly be described as such. But when I think of the *lefse* of my childhood, comparing it in size to a pancake would have been as ludicrous as comparing a wagon wheel to a silver dollar. The *lefse* my mother made was baked directly on the surface of her black cast-iron range, and each piece was a tremendous circle of some twenty-four inches in diameter. Its construction was a lesson in patience, dexterity, and in hoodwinking the pull of gravity. It was not only the pièce de résistance of our winter holidays, but its preparation was a ritual that consumed an entire day.

Early in the morning, my mother boiled a large kettle of potatoes, mashed them, added cream, butter, salt, and pepper, and put them out on the back porch to chill for a couple of hours. Meanwhile, she prepared the top of the range for the baking. She rubbed it vigorously with a crumpled newspaper to smooth it, and then she rubbed it clean with a damp cloth. The coals were encouraged to burn down to an ash, because an active flame would make the surface too hot.

Now the chilled potatoes were brought in, and a judicious amount of flour was added. The flour was the tricky part. If too much flour was added the *lefse* would be tough, and if too little was added the *lefse* would fall apart on the way from the rolling board to the range, which was a good ten-foot walk. Taking the position that she could add to the dough easier than she could subtract, my mother went easy on the flour the first time around. Then she broke off a piece of dough about the size of an orange and rolled it thin on her great metal rolling board that pulled out of her cabinet. A thick piece of *lefse* was the sign of a slaggardly housewife and was not to be tolerated. When the giant two-foot circle was as thin as the law allowed, my mother went to the window and pulled out the wooden rod at the bottom of the window shade which, fortuitously, happened to be exactly the right length for turning *lefse*. It had already been sharpened and smoothed from previous bakings and was always stored back in its original place. (On the frontier, everything, ideally, had a multiple use.)

My mother carefully rolled the circle of dough about three-quarters of the way up on the curtain rod and then carried it across the kitchen to the range. It was a perilous trip. If she had put enough flour in the dough, she made the trip successfully. (If she had not, the dough that was hanging from the rod fell to the floor.) Having reached the range, she unrolled the dough on it. She let it bake a minute or two, and when it began to bubble slightly, she slid the curtain rod under the center of the *lefse,* lifted it up, and turned it on the other side. The first turning was always the critical one. If there was not quite enough flour in the dough, the *lefse* might also fall apart at this point. The first *lefse* rarely turned out perfectly, and this was all right with us children. My mother always let us eat this one immediately. We divided it among us, slathered it with butter, and had a pre-holiday feast.

Now the *serious* baking began. My mother walked back and forth from cabinet to range for hours, rolling and baking. Each *lefse* took about five minutes to bake and had to be turned at least a dozen times. My mother's face was soon smudged with flour and her apron and the floor around the range covered with brown flour dust, because the top of the range had to be brushed off after each baking. But at the end of the day she had several dozen beautiful, perfect circles of brown-flecked *lefse* piled up on a dish towel. To serve the *lefse,* she cut each piece into eight pie-shaped wedges with scissors, buttered the wedges, rolled them up, and arranged them on a platter.

Mashed potatoes and tiny, nutmeggy meatballs in gravy were always served with the *lefse* and, if it was available, *lutefisk.* Norwegian cod steeped in white lye, *lutefisk* is what every red-blooded 100 percent Norwegian is supposed to be wild about. The prairie grocers usually ordered it by the barrel for the winter holidays. Secretly, I hated it. It had to be boiled before serving, and it came out of the water slippery and tricky, with dangerous little bones that could stick in a child's throat. But I always ate a token morsel and never said a word. A child of Norway not liking *lutefisk*! Heresy.

No arm twisting was necessary, however, to get me to eat *rømmegrøt*, the legendary cream porridge that Norwegians call their national porridge and whose recipe reportedly has been handed down from generation to generation for centuries. Floating in drawn butter, it is a dish so divine that one can easily visualize the Scandinavian Gods Odin and Thor relishing it from golden spoons. Definitely a meal in itself and then some, it was a dish my mother often served when unexpected relatives dropped in around suppertime (there were no telephones on the prairies to warn one of unexpected guests) and she wanted to serve them something very special.

This is how my mother made it. She poured a quart of thick sour cream into a frying pan and boiled it for about five minutes to reduce it, then sifted half a cup of flour over it and continued to boil it until bubbles of butter could be seen around the edges. Next she began to stir vigorously with a wooden spoon until she could tip the pan slightly and ladle out some of the butter. My mother stirred and ladled, and stirred and ladled, until finally she had a cream pitcher filled with beautiful drawn butter. Left in the pan was the moist golden curd.

Setting this aside, my mother scalded six cups of milk in a large kettle, then sifted a cup of flour, three tablespoons of sugar, and a tablespoon of salt into the milk and beat vigorously until she had a smooth sauce. Finally, the curd left in the frying pan was added, and another five or ten minutes of hard beating was required before the curd disappeared smoothly into the mixture. The porridge was now ready. It smelled fabulous—like something straight out of a Sigrid Undset saga.

The *rømmegrøt* was poured onto dinner plates and sprinkled with sugar and cinnamon, after which the drawn butter was poured over it until it formed a golden rim around the plate. Absolutely nothing else was served with it—except a glass of milk. Tradition held that one must drink milk with *rømmegrøt*!

When I describe this meal to my non-Norwegian friends they often ask, "Didn't you get hungry before you went to bed?" And I always reply, "If you are ever able to work your entire way around a dinner plate of *rømmegrøt*, I guarantee you that you will not be hungry for another twelve, fifteen, make that twenty-four hours."

As a matter of fact, the ability to eat any quantity of *rømmegrøt* had to be learned in stages. As toddlers we took a teaspoon or two from our mother's plate as we sat on her lap. As six-year-olds we could handle a saucerful.

*Nothing to Do but Stay*

At ten we could manage a salad plate, and as young teen-agers we graduated to a luncheon plate. When we could ultimately digest a full dinner plate of *rømmegrøt* at one sitting without faltering, we knew our adolescence had ended and we were adults.

The sharing of food was a way of life on the prairies. It was shared with joy and laughter in health and with love and concern in time of illness. A case in point is the fa-mous incident of my mother's chicken soup. The time was the harsh winter of the great influenza epidemic in 1919. My mother already had three children under the age of five and another under the apron. As the flu raged across the country, farm families in the community quarantined themselves. The men went to town only to replenish es-sential supplies. But late in March, when the winter bliz-zards were at their worst, my father came down with a severe case of the flu and was bedridden. My mother had to milk the cows as well as feed and water the horses and other livestock. The pump at the windmill kept freezing up, and she had to pour boiling water down the casing to thaw the ice. It was a desperate time.

One day the mail carrier, who was the only outside con-tact my mother had, told her that her cousin Tomas's fam-ily, who lived a mile down the road, had also been struck with the flu. Ingeborg, the mailman reported, had been flat on her back for ten days and was getting weaker and weaker because she could swallow neither food nor water.

My mother anguished for a way in which she could help. She did what she could do. She went out to the chicken coop and managed to catch two roosters, chopped their heads off, cleaned and boiled them, and made a rich chicken soup. She poured it into a half-gallon canning jar and sealed it. Then she went out to the barn, harnessed up a pair of horses, hitched them to the box sled, and drove over the snow-packed roads to her neighbors' farm. She pressed the jar of chicken soup into Tomas's hands, turned the horses around, and hurried home to her family.

Now Ingeborg takes over the telling of the story. Ingeborg reported that when her husband came to the bedroom with the jar of soup and lifted off the lid, she smelled the aroma of the chicken soup and suddenly became so ravenously hungry that she sat up in bed, seized the jar, and drank deeply.

It was the first nourishment she had been able to swallow for days. From that moment on she gained strength and soon was well.

A robust woman with a ringing laugh, Ingeborg was a marvelous storyteller, and by the time I was born and had grown old enough to hear the story, it had already become a classic. Each time Ingeborg told the story, she drank more of the soup than the time before. When she had recounted the story for twenty years, she was consuming the entire half gallon at once!

# 4

## The Last Turkey

*Roast turkey was not a staple at our Thanksgiving* dinners when I was a child. I can remember, in fact, only one Thanksgiving on which we had turkey, and the path by which this rare bird landed on our holiday table was a convoluted one.

Because we lived in a Norwegian-American community, turkey was one thing we could live without on Thanksgiving. What we couldn't live without were *lutefisk* and *lefse*. As long as we had an abundance of these and other Nordic dishes, who needed turkey? Besides, we couldn't afford to buy one; no farmers in the vicinity raised turkeys.

One spring, however, when I was about eight, my

mother made what she considered a very sage decision: she decided to go into the turkey business. She had observed the previous November that the meat markets in Williston were getting what she termed "land office prices" for dressed turkey, and she thought she would be wise to get in on the ground floor of this bonanza.

My father was horrified. He said that he not only despised the taste of turkey, he hated the looks of the birds, and if she brought one of them on the place, it would be more or less over his dead body. My mother replied soothingly that he had nothing to worry about; it would be her own personal little money-making project, and she would never ask him to pluck as much as a pin feather off those valuable dressed birds she would take to market in a year or two.

My mother already had a hundred or more chickens, whose eggs she traded every week for groceries at the Williston markets. The thing to do, she said, was to set some fertile turkey eggs under one of her Plymouth Rock chickens. After the hen had sat on those eggs for four weeks, my mother conjectured, she wouldn't have the heart not to accept the baby turkeys, even though they didn't look like what normally hatched in her nest.

The next time my mother was in town she inquired around at the markets and secured the name of a woman in another township who raised Bronze turkeys. The woman reluctantly sold my mother eight fertile turkey

*Nothing to Do but Stay*

eggs for fifty cents apiece. The reason the price was so high, she said, was that fertile turkey eggs were scarce as hen's teeth and valuable as gold.

My mother chose for her new project one of her broodiest Plymouth Rock hens, who was already sitting, blissfully unaware of the vile deception that was about to be perpetrated upon her, on her own eggs, which she had painstakingly laid—day after day—until she had a clutch of ten. Every time the hen came off her nest and went out into the barnyard to get food and water and to bathe in the dust, my mother crept into the chicken coop and replaced one of her eggs with a turkey egg. After a few days the chicken was sitting, all unknowing, on completely foreign goods.

Now all my mother had to worry about was whether this hen might have a built-in calendar on which she was ticking off the days until hatching time; the incubation period for chicken eggs is twenty-two days, but for turkey eggs it is twenty-eight. The hen had already sat at least a week on her own eggs before my mother began switching them. It was possible that if she didn't feel some live action under her after two or three more weeks she would tire of the entire business and abandon her nest.

But my mother had picked the right chicken; although she became very pale around the comb and developed a harried look in her eyes, she doggedly stuck to her nest for four weeks. When the hatching finally began and the large dark-gray turkey poults broke out of their shells, she didn't go into shock or show any outward signs of trauma, whatever mixed feelings might have been churning within her.

Only six out of the eight eggs hatched, however, and my mother quickly learned that baby turkeys were not made of the sturdy stuff of baby chicks; they came out of the nest fragile and wobbly. My mother hurriedly set up a wire nursery behind the coal range in the kitchen for a week. She spent hours trying to teach the poults to eat, coaxing them with mashed hard-boiled egg yolks and dry oatmeal. When she put the hen out in the barnyard with her strange little flock, she had another problem. The other hens who were parading around with their flocks of yellow baby chicks became enraged when they saw the big dark foreign-looking poults, and they flew at them and pecked them on the heads. This aroused the ire of the foster mother, and she attacked the other hens. There was a battle royal, chicken feathers flying in all directions. My mother managed to rescue the turkey poults and locked them in a wire pen in the barn, together with the mother hen, for several more weeks until they were old enough to withstand attack.

Only four out of the six poults survived until they were full-grown, but luckily three of them turned out to be hens and one a gobbler. My mother decided that this combination put her squarely in the turkey business. When spring came, all she had to do, she said, was let her three hens sit on their own eggs and by the following Thanksgiving she would have several dozen lovely turkeys to take to market.

It didn't turn out to be quite that easy. The turkey hens refused to have anything to do with the ready-made box nests in the chicken coop, and by the middle of April they were beginning to lay their eggs in weird places. My mother would find an egg in the horse manger, or in one of the cow stalls, or under the mailbox, or behind the granary. Whenever my mother found an egg she would snatch it up, fearful that another animal would break it or eat it, and she would take it indoors for safekeeping. She soon realized, though, that the reason the turkey hen never laid her egg in the same place twice was that she thought her nest had been violated when she didn't find her previous day's egg there. The next time my mother found a turkey egg in what she considered a reasonably adequate place for nesting, she replaced it with a chicken egg; when my mother returned to the spot the next day, there was a new turkey egg beside the chicken egg. My mother again took the turkey egg and replaced it with a chicken egg. She followed this procedure until there were about fourteen eggs in the nest, and when the turkey hen began showing signs that she wanted to settle down on the nest and brood, my mother one day took away all of the chicken eggs and gave the hen back her own turkey eggs.

By the middle of May my mother had one turkey hen sitting under a cottonwood tree in the small grove at the northern edge of the farm; the second hen was warming her clutch of eggs under a strawstack in the wheatfield; and the third one was nesting in the iron forge in my father's blacksmith shop.

Despite their offbeat nesting places, the turkey hens had wonderful hatches that year, each of them coming out with a dozen or more poults, most of which made it through the crucial first weeks. The turkey gobbler, rightfully enough, took credit for the entire lot. The hour before sundown each evening he would run his three hens and their offspring together on the grassy clearing between the house and barn; then he would strut for the benefit of animal and human spectators alike. First he fanned out his tail to its full magnificence; then he would blow out his chest and puff; make a wide circle, blow out his chest, and puff; circle in the opposite direction, blow out his chest, and puff. Watching him, the half-grown male turkeys would emulate him, even though they had very little tail and not much chest with which to work. It was the closest we ever came on the farm to a circus.

By midsummer, just about the time my mother was given to standing around the barnyard admiring her handsome new flock and making remarks like, "There's nothing to raising turkeys," the birds turned on her, determined to prove her wrong.

*Nothing to Do but Stay*

They began to run away from home.

One day my father returned from town, burst into the house, and said he had spotted the entire "tribe," which was the most deleterious word he could think of for a group of anything, eating the heads off the ripening wheat in a neighbor's field.

"If I ever see a turkey in that field again," he said, "every one of the tribe goes on the chopping block."

A strong and for the most part silent man, my father never made idle threats; my mother knew he meant business. She forthwith dispatched my ten-year-old sister Fran and me, armed with brooms, to chase the turkeys out of the forbidden field; from that day on we were assigned what became the most onerous task of our childhoods: herding turkeys.

We soon learned that turkeys are congenitally indisposed to the principle of herding. Neither are they compatible with chasing, shooing, or rounding up. All of our other farm animals had the homing instinct. Our horses could find their way home blindfolded in a snowstorm. Our cows could break out and wander miles from home, but as soon as they saw our car they would lift up their heads and run unerringly in the direction of home. Our chickens had the good sense never to leave home in the first place. But once turkeys have left home, they have never heard of it; when approached on foreign soil they will panic, break rank, and skitter in every direction ex-

*The Last Turkey*                                            93

cept homeward. That first day it had taken Fran and me hours of broom waving and shouting to bring my mother's turkeys a quarter of a mile home, and before we got them there we had crisscrossed several public roads and invaded a few other neighbors' wheatfields as well.

For the remainder of the summer, my mother said, it would be our job "to keep track of the turkeys." She emphasized that it was far from a full-time job and that our brother and three older sisters had other things to do. Just wherever Fran and I were—from sunup to sundown—we must "keep the turkeys in mind." Just know where they are at all times. And if you don't see them, grab your brooms and start looking. It was all right for them to stray into the forty-acre cow pasture, but if we saw them heading toward the line fence, we must run like wild and try to head them back home. It seemed that every time we had settled down to read a book or had a good hopscotch game going, someone would shout, "Have you seen the turkeys lately?" and we must be off with our brooms to attempt to rout several dozen birds who resisted chasing as they feinted this way and that, stretched their necks and retracted them, made garbled noises, and—if all else failed—flew over our heads.

By the end of the summer Fran and I were praying that my mother would quit raising turkeys, but that fall she took a couple of dozen plump dressed turkeys to the Williston markets and made what she considered a nice

*Nothing to Do but Stay*

profit. My father butchered them for her, which was the only job in the turkey line he was willing to undertake and which, considering his regard for the birds, probably gave him a certain satisfaction. My mother cleaned and dressed the turkeys herself, and Fran and I helped pluck pin feathers—a job that ranked, after herding, as our least favorite occupation.

For the next four summers, during which we grew from children into our teens, Fran and I watched out for my mother's turkeys, and at the point where we began to think that we would surely grow old and still be herding, the word came unexpectedly. Said my mother out of the blue one bright autumn day, "I don't think it pays to raise turkeys anymore. I'm selling out."

And the week before Thanksgiving sell out she did. What is more, in a rare burst of hang-the-expense abandon, she kept the choicest young turkey for our own Thanksgiving.

After years of doing battle with it on the wing, Fran and I had our first taste of turkey. My father voiced the opinion, as he helped himself to *lutefisk* and *lefse,* that we wouldn't like it.

"I tasted turkey once," he said. "Once was enough for me."

Fran and I couldn't decide whether we liked it. It had a strange, rather dry nutlike taste, compared to chicken. After we had cleansed our palates with generous helpings of mashed potatoes and Norwegian meatballs in gravy, we decided, yes, we might try just another bite of turkey. It tasted better the second time around.

But my sister and I confided to each other that the happiest part of that Thanksgiving day was not the good food but the thought that next summer we'd be free.

Free as birds. Free as the birds that fly high in the sky, that is.

# 5

# Ole and Anna

*Ole was not your typical avuncular sort, about* whom a child would say smugly to a friend, "You know, he's my uncle." Just looking at Ole, in fact, put the fear of God into me. His bleary eyes crowding a long thin nose could roll alarmingly up into his skinny head, which frequently shook back and forth with uncontrolled laughter. Loose-jointed and tall, he walked with a curious flat-footed yet swinging gait, and he had an awesome right hand that was misshapen from a bullet wound received in his youth, when he carelessly rested his palm on the barrel end of a loaded rifle. Still, growing up on the North Dakota prairies was less desolate because my uncle lived on the farm catty-corner across the road from us. It was comforting on a cold winter's night to look out the window and see Ole's lamp light shining through the darkness.

Ole was not a trailblazer. He had followed my mother out to North Dakota only after she was well settled on her homestead with husband and children, and he had been lucky enough to acquire the 160-acre farm across from hers, where there was already a small house and barn. He had bought the farm for an uncommonly low cash payment from the original homesteader, a friend of his who was anxious to sell out and return to Minnesota.

My mother was not easy about this arrangement. Ole had become the enfant terrible of the family, even though he was the oldest of seven children of Norwegian immigrants who had settled on a Minnesota farm in the early 1880s. Until he decided to come to North Dakota he had never shown any ambition to better himself but was content to live at home with his parents and hire out occasionally as a farmhand. It wasn't until his early thirties that he had been persuaded by a misguided companion to take his first drink of *brennevin*—which instantly opened up to the previously sober Ole a life of such gay camaraderie in one saloon after another that he regretted the rest of his life that he had misspent the early years of his adulthood ignorant of life's real pleasures.

My mother already had three children and another on the way; she took the position that she had enough re-

*Nothing to Do but Stay*

sponsibilities without taking on the job of warden to her forty-eight-year-old brother. And there was another reason for my mother's apprehension. To make up the cash payment with which to buy his farm, Ole had gone to see their youngest sister Marya, who worked as a housekeeper for a farmer in eastern North Dakota, and he had sweet-talked her out of four hundred dollars of her life's savings —an amount she had accumulated after years of frugality and hard work. Ole had solemnly sworn to Marya—and when he was solemn he could be as convincing as a circuit preacher—that he would not only pay her back with his first wheat crop, but that he would add on a *prinselig* rate of interest, she could count on that.

Perhaps because she had always taken a more jaundiced view of life than her younger sister (and perhaps because she knew their brother better), my mother feared mightily that Marya would never see her four hundred dollars again—let alone the princely interest. The transaction having been made, however, there was nothing my mother could do about it, except to watch Ole take possession of his farm. She baked his bread and washed his clothes and cleaned his house when she could no longer stand the sight of it. And she worried about him and about Marya. Instead of paying back his sister with the money from his first wheat crop, which he had let out on shares because he had no farm equipment, Ole bought a spring wagon and a handsome pair of sorrel draft horses with silvery manes and tails. With his second year's crop he bought a plow, a harrow, and a binder. That wasn't Marya's year either. With his third crop he bought four cows, a bull, and a DeLaval cream separator. Nothing left for Marya that year. The fourth year he bought a field mower, a hay rake, another cow, and a flock of Rhode Island Reds.

He no longer mentioned Marya.

He told my mother often, though, that he was well satisfied with his life on the prairies; he could come and go as he wished and he didn't have to answer to a living soul— *en levende sjel,* he would say, rolling his eyes up into his head and pounding his battered fist on the table.

At least once a week Ole's spring wagon and sorrels could be seen tied to the hitching post in front of the pool halls in one or another of the nearby towns. Ostensibly pool halls, they were actually saloons. Although North Dakota had been dry since statehood in 1889, enforcement of the liquor laws was practically nonexistent in the territory west of the Missouri River up until 1920, when Prohibition was enacted.

Any time between dark and midnight my mother and father would hear Ole coming home, singing at the top of his lungs and roaring at his horses, who were galloping crazily in the traces and whinnying into the night as they carried their master home.

Unless he had to go to town on an unexpected errand

(in which case he was lured into the saloon like the sailor to the Sirens) Ole liked to stay at home on Saturday because he wanted to be clear-headed on Sunday morning to go to church, the white steeple of which was plainly visible from the front room of his house. He always had my mother launder his white Sunday shirt. Sitting on the hard backless church bench with his arms crossed against his chest, Ole listened to the minister warn of the perils of drinking in illegal saloons and getting into the wrong kind of company, and his chin would rise thoughtfully up in the air as his face became creased with solemnity. Every now and then he rolled his eyes and looked from side to side, and suddenly he would clear his throat with a great guttural "arrumph!" One month out of the year he took his turn as sexton, coming early on Sunday morning to fire the furnace and to ring the great bell in the tower.

The church was hard put to meet operating expenses, even though the minister was shared with three other rural churches in the territory. One year when Christmas rolled around, the elders, of whom Ole was one, discovered the coffers were so bare they couldn't even buy the tree that was traditionally set up in church for the children's program the Sunday evening before Christmas. The wheat crop had been very poor the previous autumn and money was scarce; the program would have to go on both without a tree and without treats for the children.

Ole went home and brooded over this sorry state of

affairs. He was fond of children, even though he always managed to frighten them with his rolling eyes and uncontrollable laughter. The day before the program, another elder of the church who lived nearby, an old man named Thomas, dropped in to see him. Thomas was the giant of the neighborhood at well over six feet, and his awesome appearance was enhanced by a head of luxuriant ruddy hair going gray and a phenomenally long beard so thick it rested on his chest like a bush. Thomas, it turned out, had also been fuming mightily at the thought of such a threadbare Christmas for the children.

As they sat at Ole's kitchen table talking and drinking coffee, Thomas suddenly struck a mammoth fist on the table and shouted, "It shall not be!" Whereupon he turned his pockets inside out, scattering coins across the table. Caught up in the drama, Ole instantly emptied his own pockets. They counted their change and decided they might, just might have enough money to buy a small Christmas tree. Jumping into Ole's spring wagon, they drove the sorrels to town, where they quickly discovered that the only Christmas tree left was a nine-foot fir leaning against the front of the hardware store. Their hearts sank; they could never afford a tree as large as that. But now they were here, they might as well ask.

The hardware dealer said he had pulled the tree along with a dozen or so smaller ones off a carload coming through from Canada; he had been unable to sell it because it was much too tall to fit in anyone's house. Now he was stuck with it, he lamented, and if Ole and Thomas would be good enough to take it off his hands he'd let them have it for pocket money. For so little pocket money, in fact, that they had enough left over to buy candy and oranges for the children.

They jubilantly loaded the tree into the spring wagon, and on the way home, as giddy as if they had stopped by the saloon, they concocted a delicious scheme.

They hid the tree in Ole's barn and spent the remainder of the day making popcorn garlands with which to festoon its branches. Ole popped the corn and Thomas, who was handier with a darning needle, threaded the long strings. Neither of them had ever done this before; the women had always done it. They groaned and swore as they burned and pricked their fingers. Darkness had fallen by the time they had finished the garlands, so they loaded the tree back into the wagon and drove quickly to the church. Parking the wagon and horses snugly behind the church and using only a small lantern with the wick turned down low, they managed to get the tree into the church and set up beside the pulpit. Then they went into the cellar, which could only be reached by a set of trapdoors behind the building, and rustled around like two moles until they found the box of antique Christmas ornaments which the congregation had collected through donations over the years.

Fearful that someone was going to drive past and see a light, they set the lantern on the floor behind the pulpit and turned it down until it was almost extinguished, and in the semidarkness they frenziedly looped the popcorn garlands around the tree and hung the ornaments. Then they quickly got the horses out from behind the church and drove stealthily home.

The next evening when the dozen families in the community drove into the churchyard with their wagons and horses for the children's program—which was to start promptly, as usual, at eight o'clock—they were consternated to find the church not only dark but locked! This could not be. Never in the history of the church had it ever been locked. Pandemonium broke loose in the churchyard, men shaking their heads, women chattering, children crying, and horses stomping. Where was Ole? December was his month to be sexton; it was his job to come early to fire the furnace and light the carbide lamps in their sconces on the walls.

Someone noticed that the windows had suddenly lit up, and then a great shout was heard. "Come in!"

Again the door was tried and found unlocked. Everyone rushed into the church, and men, women, and children alike stopped dead in their tracks. At the front of the church, in the eerie light of the carbide lamps, stood the weirdest Christmas tree they had ever seen. Incredibly skinny and tall, reaching for the rafters, it looked as if it

*Nothing to Do but Stay*

*Ole Gafkjen and bearded Thomas Walstad with their surprise Christmas tree. From the author's collection.*

had been decorated and then hit by a sudden windstorm. The popcorn garlands hung haphazardly in great loops from the branches; the crystal balls, the wooden figurines, and all of the other ornaments were wildly askew, as if they had been aimed from several feet away and had landed at random. The treetop angel was hanging on its stomach from the highest branch, its snowy wings spread out as though it were trying to take flight.

As the congregation gazed, hypnotized, out from behind the pulpit sprang two figures, one tall and the other impossibly tall, wearing winter overcoats and four-buckle arctics. The giant was rumbling and shaking his long beard back and forth like an outsized St. Nicholas, and the other one was rolling his eyes up into his head and laughing outrageously.

*"Gledelig jul!"* they shouted. "Merry Christmas!"

Each year afterward the story of Ole and Thomas and the crazy Christmas tree was told, until it became a legend in its time. I myself grew up with the legend, because the actual event occurred three years before I was born.

The onset of Prohibition in the 1920s changed the course of Ole's life. It was very depressing for him to go to town and see the saloon boarded up; there was nowhere he could sit around and talk with old acquaintances—*gamle kjente.* The nearby small towns did not traffic in illegal liquor, at least in the first years, and a person had to go to Williston—almost thirty miles away—to have any hope of finding bootleg whiskey. Ole seldom got to Williston because he didn't as yet own an automobile. He tried to brew his own beer, and he usually had a ten-gallon crock of mash bubbling under the hot-water reservoir of his cast-iron range, but he was not very good at it; it frequently went sour, and even if he was able now and then to turn out a good batch his game hand made him clumsy at bottling and sealing the brew. What is more, there was always the threat of revenuers, and on occasion both he and my father, when they had been in town and had heard rumors of federal agents in the territory, would rush home, get their crocks out from under the range, carry them out, and dump the contents behind their cottonwood trees.

The grocery stores, especially during the long winter months, became the place where men could meet and pass the time of day. There were two grocers in Appam. One was in the business of selling groceries; the other had a few items in the front of the store but was much more interested in the pinochle or penny-ante poker game that was generally going on beside the potbellied coal heater in the back. When he was in the middle of a game, the grocer would become furious if a customer came in the door and actually had the temerity to ask for a can of beans or a hunk of Limburger cheese.

Card playing was not one of Ole's vices; he said he could

never get the hang of it. But for want of anything else to do in the winter months he'd often stand around and watch the game. He would walk around the players and look at their cards, and sometimes what he saw would make him roll his eyes up into his head and look very solemn, and he would give his loud guttural sitting-in-church "arrumph!" At other times what he saw would elicit an attack of uncontrollable laughter.

It made the players nervous. One day they began a running joke with Ole that went on for weeks. Why didn't he get himself a housekeeper now that there was so little reason for him to come to town? The first time it was mentioned Ole laughed so long and hard that the grocer had to go to the front of the store and get him a glass of buttermilk to quiet him.

The next week when Ole looked in on the game, the players started in on him again. How long had Ole lived on that *gudsforlatt* farm by himself now? Six years? Wasn't it about time he deserved some good home-cooking for a change instead of living on a steady diet of bologna and summer sausage? Why, if Ole had a *huskeeper,* he could live like a gentleman—like a *dannet mann.*

This time Ole didn't laugh quite so hard.

The banter went on for weeks, until one early spring day the cardplayers greeted him with the joyful news that they had finally solved his problem. One of them had gotten the address, he said, of a dandy little lady in the eastern part of the state who was looking for work. She had been born in Norway and had come over with her brother and his family when she was a little girl, and now she wanted to go out to work on her own. The best part of it was, the players said, that she still spoke nothing but Norwegian, so she wouldn't be able to give him any back talk in English, and she was reported to be a very fine cook and could bake all of his favorite Norwegian foods.

"How would you like to eat *lefse* and *klubbe* every day, Ole?" one of the players asked. This time Ole rolled his eyes and looked solemn.

One day after he had finished his spring seeding, Ole came over to see my mother, and he looked so serious that she thought he must have lost his favorite brindle cow. He told my mother that the time had come when he *must* have a housekeeper. He could no longer tolerate, he said, living like a slattern—like a *sjusket kvinne*. He had been looking around, and he had had the most amazing good fortune to locate a *huskeeper* with the finest recommendations, and as a matter of fact she was coming in on tonight's train.

Startled out of her wits, my mother blurted out the first thing that came into her mind. "But, Ole, where will she sleep? Your house is so small!"

It was true that Ole's house had just two rooms—a front room and a kitchen—unless you counted the tiny attic loft that could only be reached by a perilously steep, almost perpendicular flight of rough steps, open on all sides, that led from a corner of the kitchen. Ole himself slept on a daybed in the front room, even though the previous owner had left in the loft an old heavy iron bedstead that he had not found worth the trouble to heave down the stairs. "That bed you should have for a wedding gift, Ole!" his friend had declared, and Ole had replied, "*That* I shall never need!" and then they had pounded each other on the back and had a last good laugh together.

Now, in answer to my mother's question, Ole said, "*Hun er ung og sprek. Hun kan sove oppe på.*" She is young and spry. She can sleep upstairs.

The next day my mother, full of trepidation, walked across the road to meet Anna, her brother's *huskeeper*. She found Ole at the kitchen table soberly drinking an uncommonly fine-looking cup of coffee in which he was dunking a crisp diamond-shaped *fattigman*—obviously fresh from the lard kettle. Standing at the coal range frying Norwegian meatballs which smelled pungently of nutmeg was a somewhat dour-faced woman of around fifty, wearing a heavily starched gingham dress covered by an even heavier starched gingham apron. She was small and squat and had thick brown hair showing not a trace of gray, parted in the center and pulled back in a tight bun. When she came forward to shake hands, she listed startlingly over on one leg. She was wearing a shoe with a thick lift, but even with its support one leg was many inches shorter than the other.

Anna invited my mother to sit up to the table for a cup of coffee and a *fattigman*. Looking around the kitchen, my mother was surprised to see that it had already been spruced up. The top of the coal range had been rubbed shiny with newspapers, and on top of the warming oven four loaves of no-nonsense bread were rising. From where she sat my mother could look into the front room and was amazed to see in what had been an empty corner a handsome curio cabinet with a curved front glass—already filled with photographs, fine crystal, china cups, and other mementos. Anna, my mother surmised, had come prepared to stay. My mother's eyes, now rapidly taking in everything, suddenly lit on the daybed. The loft! Anna could never have climbed that treacherous flight of steps last night.

Instantly reading my mother's mind, Anna said with a short laugh that she had managed that stairway quite well for her first night and she was confident that she would do even better tonight. The thing to do, she said, was to go up facing forward and to come down *baklengs,* backward.

Six months to the day later, according to my mother, Ole came rushing into our house and cried, *"Vi må bli gift!"* We must be married.

My mother said it sounded for all the world as if he had gotten Anna "into trouble" and that there was a shotgun at his back, but she quickly realized that this was not a possibility. Ole said that he and Anna were going to be married the next Saturday at the minister's house in town, and they were. Anna wore her brown Sunday dress with the brown beads that reached below her waist, and Ole wore, along with his deadliest expression, the new blue serge suit he had purchased for the occasion. My parents and all six of their children witnessed the ceremony, and afterward my mother invited all of the relatives on her side of the family, numbering some twenty-five, home for a buffet supper. Then Ole and Anna walked home, Ole carefully parting for his wife the two sets of barbed-wire fences that they must climb through to get from our farm to theirs. Ole must also have managed to negotiate the perilous steps to the loft that night, because he never again slept on the daybed in the front room. The next day Anna had him move it out to the back porch.

For a man of fifty-five, Ole trained remarkably well. About the house and barn he soon became as fussy as his wife. The cows had to be milked and the eggs picked up from under the Rhode Island Reds exactly twelve hours apart morning and evening. The milk had to be separated from the cream in the DeLaval separator at just the right speed—not turning the handle too fast or too slow. Exactly three-quarters of a dipper of water, no more and no less, must be poured into the separator to rinse out the residual cream. The clothes were washed on Monday—with Ole pumping the water from the cistern for the oval washboiler—ironed on Tuesday, and mended on Wednesday. The butter was churned on Thursday and the bread and cookies baked on Friday.

In the evening they sat in the front room at the heavy oak dining-room table that Anna had had shipped up from eastern North Dakota; Anna crocheted or tatted while Ole read *Den Decorah-Posten*, the Norwegian newspaper published out of Iowa. Delicate lace curtains hung at the windows, intricate stitched samplers decorated the walls, and a mammoth green fern proliferated in a corner.

Everything was well ordered—until Ole, years after his neighbors had become motorized, decided to buy a truck. Which enabled him to acquire, now and then, some moonshine whiskey. Which sent the well-ordered life across the road haywire. My mother would know the worst if Ole hadn't arrived home by sundown. She could be certain that if she didn't go across the road to see Anna, Anna would soon be laboriously climbing, with her bad leg, the two sets of barbed-wire fences that separated our farms. Limping heavily up to the house, her face set in hard misery, she would say in Norwegian, "My man has gone to town and got himself into *bad compahnee* and now the cows are crying because their udders hurt and I cannot milk them all myself."

Anna had steadfastly refused to learn to speak English, even though she had come over from Norway with her brother's family at the age of twelve. She always insisted that she didn't understand a word of it either, which we took with a grain of salt; she had picked up some key English phrases which she used very effectively. One of these was "bad company." She always vowed that it wasn't Ole's fault when he went to town and drank too much, because he would have been perfectly fine if *bad compahnee* hadn't led him astray.

My mother would always take pity on Anna and the cows (my father said let the cows' udders burst and it will teach Ole a lesson), and she would walk back with Anna and help her with the milking. And the egg picking. And the cream separating. Even under adverse circumstances, Anna still had to do everything just right.

In the early morning hours Ole would generally come roaring home in his truck, simultaneously shifting and clutching and braking, stripping the gears and making a terrible noise. Even when he was sober he had never learned how to operate his truck with any facility, and when he had been drinking all of his reflexes forsook him.

What happened after Ole entered his house no one ever knew. Although Anna complained bitterly to my mother about Ole's staying out and carousing, which was the fault of *bad compahnee,* she never said a word about what happened after Ole came home. My mother at first wor-

*Nothing to Do but Stay*

ried that Anna couldn't hold her own against her husband when he was in his cups, but because Anna never spoke about it my mother decided she must have worked it out in her own way. My mother speculated that Anna might simply retire to the loft, possibly with rolling pin in hand, and if Ole attempted to climb those treacherous steps a mere tap with the rolling pin would send him flying. There was one thing in Anna's favor. Ole had never been heard to say a cross or mean word to or about his wife; it was possible that this held over when he had been drinking. In town, however, he often became so combative that he was thrown out in the streets, after which he would occasionally stop at our house and try to pick a fight with my mother. Unless my father was at home. No matter "how far gone he was in drink," as my mother put it, he instinctively knew when my father was at home, in which case he gave our farm a wide berth.

Unfelicitously, Anna had taken the occasion of her wedding day to tell my mother that she hoped we six children wouldn't be running back and forth across the road all of the time. If there was anyone who could take a hint it was my mother, and in future years she forbade us to visit Ole and Anna unless we had a definite mission. If my father had butchered, she would send us down with a succulent piece of calf liver or some fresh sausage, or she would dispatch us to invite Ole and Anna for Christmas eve supper or Easter dinner. And if she desperately needed something—such as a cake of yeast or a box of kitchen matches or a quart of flour, she would send us down to borrow. My mother figured that for all of the things she did for Anna—her spring and fall housecleaning, her interior painting and her grocery shopping, not to mention milking the cows when Ole got into bad company—the least Anna could do was to lend her a few things once in a while.

How I hated this borrowing journey. When I became old enough to climb through two barbed-wire fences and cross the road by myself, there was nothing for it but that I must take my turn. First the message had to be memorized in Norwegian and in a loud voice, because when it came to lending, Anna, always rather deaf, turned deaf as a house.

"Mama wonders if you would be so kind as to lend her a cup of sugar." *"Mama undres om du vil vaere så snill å la henna ha en kopp sukker."*

This sentence was rehearsed time and again at home and repeated as I climbed through the fences. When I knocked on the door it was answered promptly, "Kum in," because Anna had more than likely been sitting at the window watching me come and had already guessed what I wanted to borrow, cup in hand. She would be standing in the middle of the kitchen, a dour smile of welcome on her face, and if Ole was home he would stand towering over us both, rolling his eyes at me and laughing. I would then repeat my sentence, in which the *du,* the *så,* the *la,* and the *ha* had become hopelessly jumbled as I climbed through the fences.

*"Hva?"* Anna would ask. *"Hva?"*

There was nothing to do but try to repeat the sentence. Then Ole, laughing uproariously now, would come to my rescue by telling Anna, rather impatiently, because he thought this charade had gone far enough, *"Sukker! Hun vil ha sukker!"*

"Yuh!" Sighing with resignation Anna would go to her cupboard and carefully measure out a cup of sugar. Then Ole would himself go to the cupboard, get out a small paper bag of candy, open it, and offer it to me. I would take out a peppermint, pop it in my mouth, say *"Mange takk,"* and retreat out the door, on the way home trying not to lose all of the sugar between the two barbed-wire fences.

Having, in his opinion, mastered the operation of a truck, Ole decided to take the bull by the horns and buy a tractor, which cut a perilous and noisy path through his fields in the following years. His neighbors for miles around always knew when Ole began plowing or planting as they heard the tractor's transmission system being pushed to the limit. Fully mechanized, Ole had no more need for his pair of spirited sorrels, and they stood idle in the barnyard for season after season. After a certain length of time Anna began trying to convince her husband that they should be sold. They were still an exceedingly handsome pair of horses and still young enough so that someone could use them for occasional farm work or for showing at fairs and parades. Ole at first cried, *"Aldri mer!"* Nevermore. Never would he part with his beautiful steeds. But the longer his wife talked the more he would—now and then—see the sense in it. For months he vacillated. He would go to town, tell the stockbuyer to come out, and then he would rush home and out to the barnyard, throw his arms around his horses, and weep hysterically. Then he would rush back to town and notify the stockbuyer that he had changed his mind.

But one day the stockbuyer came out unexpectedly, found Ole in a receptive frame of mind, and actually loaded up the horses and drove off with them. Instantly stricken with remorse, Ole hurled himself into his truck and headed for the Appam saloon (Prohibition had ended, the longest thirteen years of Ole's life), and he didn't come home for three days.

A few years later, Anna talked him into selling his cows, which threw him into such a swift and terrible depression that the only cure was to alternately mourn and celebrate for weeks. After this was over, Anna sighed and said grimly, "The chickens we are going to keep. I cannot go through this *stri*—this struggle—one more time."

When Ole was eighty-one years old, his youngest brother, who was only in his middle sixties, died unexpectedly of a heart attack back in Minnesota. I had married and was living in Ohio, but I happened to be visiting my parents at home on the farm, and my mother and I decided to make the seven-hundred-mile train trip to the funeral. Ole made up his mind to go, too, but he wanted to go a day early so that he would have time to visit with *gamle kjente* from his youth. Anna was not easy about his making the trip at his advanced age and sitting up all night on the train, but Ole was adamant, so she put a clean shirt in a box, tied it with string, and let him go.

When my mother and I arrived at the funeral home the morning before the funeral, which was to take place at the Lutheran church at one o'clock that afternoon, we found Ole standing at the bier, sobbing and blowing his nose as he looked down at his baby brother in his coffin. The tears were spattering out and falling on his brother like warm raindrops. The sight of us seemed to intensify his grief, and without even stopping to greet us he rushed from the room. A half hour later he returned and greeted us expansively, rolling his eyes at us and laughing, obviously feeling much, much better. My mother and I knew instantly where he had been.

"Why in the world," my mother whispered to me, "would they put a *saloon* next to a funeral parlor?"

Ole again walked to the bier and looked into the casket. Instantly great tears splashed out and dripped over his baby brother; Ole sobbed, blew his nose, could stand it no longer, and lunged for the door.

My mother was distraught. "Mark my words," she said, "he will never last out until the church services at one o'clock. That's two long hours from now and by then he will be far gone in drink. He will disgrace the family this time, there is no way out."

She hadn't counted on the Lutheran Ladies Aid. At 11:30 a venerable representative of the Aid entered the funeral chapel in which we were standing with a smattering of relatives and friends. She was a tall stout woman with straw-colored hair and a list in one eye. She smoothed her ample gingham apron down over her corn-flowered silk dress and announced in a high bright voice that one and all were invited to an early luncheon in the church basement, after which we would all repair upstairs to the chancel for the funeral services. Apparently not satisfied that she had rustled up enough mourners to feed, she then went next door to the saloon, hesitated a few minutes, then bravely parted the swinging doors and repeated her announcement in a loud tremulous voice.

From later accounts, it was treated with dead silence. The lady was about to retreat when she spotted Ole at the bar, instantly recognizing him not only as a relative of the deceased but as a *gamle kjente* from her youth. She rushed up to him, and they renewed acquaintanceship with much crying and giddy laughter on both sides. Ignoring the evil-eyed stares of the other patrons, the lady dragged Ole, albeit unsteadily, out of the saloon and down the street to the church basement, where she personally heaped his plate with all of his favorite Norwegian delicacies—*lefse,* mashed potatoes and gravy, meatballs, and *klubbe.* Ole partook so heartily of the fare, including many cups of strong coffee, that by the time church services started he was able to sit with my mother and nod peacefully through the entire proceedings.

On the train home that night, with Ole safely tucked away and snoring in the seat behind us, my mother gave a huge sigh of relief over the way events of the day had turned out and vowed she would never complain about a living soul again.

As an afterthought she said, "Would you ever have thought a member of the Ladies Aid would have had the gall to go into a saloon looking for customers?"

◆

My mother's relatives, clucking their tongues, often speculated why Ole found it unnecessary to repay the four hundred dollars he had borrowed from Marya to buy his farm.

My mother herself refused to speculate or even talk about it, because she knew—had always known—exactly why.

"It's just the way he is," she said.

The hard fact remained that for thirty-five years Marya tried to collect the loan without success. It wasn't as if Ole thought she didn't need the money, because several years after she lent it to him she married a widower with five children and in just a short time they had six of their own. At intervals she would write to him and ask him for it, but he never answered her letters. Three or four times over the years she made the three-hundred-mile trip up from eastern North Dakota to see him, with the express purpose of confronting him about the loan in person. But face to face, she always lost her nerve. Ole would greet her with open arms, rolling his eyes and laughing and exclaiming how happy he was to see her and telling her how uncommonly young and pretty she looked and, well, the subject never came up.

When Ole died at eighty-four he still hadn't paid his sister back—not one red cent, as Marya had often written my mother.

In the absence of a will, the court appointed my father executor of Ole's estate. Ole was far from a rich man, but poorer men have died. He left a good 160-acre farm, free and clear, no outstanding debts (except one), and several thousand dollars in the bank.

*Nothing to Do but Stay*

Anna told my father that the first thing he must do was to see that Marya got back her four hundred dollars.

"Long enough she has waited," Anna said grimly.

No one in the family dreamed that Anna knew.

My father wrote to Marya and asked her if she had a note of any kind. Marya sent him a scrap of paper, yellowed with age, on which thirty-seven years ago Ole had hastily scrawled out an IOU.

My father sent Marya the four hundred dollars. Now old herself, she wasn't all that ecstatic at receiving it. The time had long since passed, she wrote back, when she could really have used the money. And besides, Marya said, even though it had made possible the purchase of a homestead and a good way of life for her prodigal brother for over a third of a century, it now seemed so *stakkarslig* —like such a wretched amount.

# 6

# A Fourth of July in
# North Dakota

*We celebrated two Independence Days when I was a* child. The first was Syttende Mai, Norway's Independence Day on the seventeenth of May, and the second was the Fourth of July.

"We" is a misnomer, because I never actually attended a Syttende Mai celebration. The men in our rural community were the only ones who observed the holiday; the women looked the other way and tried to ignore it. My father and my uncle Ole would go to town and spend the day with the other Norwegian patriots convivially lifting glasses to Gamle Norge and, as the day wore on, emotionally swearing deathless allegiance to the beautiful Old

Country, on which most of them—the sons of immigrants —had never laid eyes.

When the Fourth of July arrived six weeks later, the men, having already had their private Independence Day celebration and still feeling good—and possibly somewhat guilty—about it, were not only willing but eager to make the Fourth a memorable day for the women and children.

My father thought of it, in fact, as a children's holiday and nostalgically recalled his own Fourth of July antics as a boy growing up in the 1890s in the verdant Red River valley of eastern North Dakota, a region quite different from the arid open prairies of the northwestern part of the state where he later homesteaded and where we now lived. He had an indulgent father who thought boys should be given a lot of freedom—especially on the Fourth of July. All three of the sons had been given bicycles, and at sunup on the morning of the Fourth they pedaled out from the family farm in opposite directions to seek out whatever excitement the nearby small towns had to offer. My father wheeled from one town to another enjoying carnivals, band concerts, horseshoe pitching, ball games, and if the day was hot, he stopped to skinny-dip in the Goose River along the way. Rounding out the day, he would end up at a dance, where he exuberantly jumped out on the dance floor and jigged. To hear my father describe it, this was an improvised dance for which no partner was required. After jigging the night away, he would pedal home

*Nothing to Do but Stay*

at dawn, meeting his brothers coming home from other directions.

Listening to my father tell of *his* childhood Fourths— which seemed to get wilder with every telling—I occasionally felt that mine were tame by comparison—although I wouldn't have traded for the world. What could beat an entire day of eating delectable hand-cranked ice cream just as it came from the freezer, and all of it absolutely free? We usually spent the day at a community picnic held at the farm of a neighbor who owned the only ice house in the territory—a happy circumstance that meant an unlimited amount of ice was available to freeze an unlimited amount of ice cream and the entire day could be dedicated to its consumption. For children who never tasted ice cream except at Christmas (when it could be frozen with ice chopped out of the water tanks at the windmill), this was a rare treat and one to which we looked forward for months ahead.

Early on the morning of the Fourth Gladys and Fran and I awoke to the popping of firecrackers and knew that Norman was sitting on the front-porch steps following his customary practice of expending his entire box of one hundred firecrackers in one glorious burst by methodically lighting one after another with kitchen matches and throwing them into the front yard.

My mother and Barney and Florence were already in the kitchen stirring up ice cream makings which we would take to the picnic. They had put a dozen eggs, three cups of sugar, and two quarts of milk into a huge kettle to simmer on the coal range and were stirring it constantly to keep it just below the boiling point. When it had congealed to the consistency of thin custard they removed it from the stove, set it outdoors to cool, added two quarts of heavy cream, and poured it into half-gallon jars. At the picnic, this would be used to make eight quarts of ice cream. They were also bringing wieners and several dozen of my mother's renowned three-day buns, which she had just removed from the oven, as well as a macaroni-salmon salad and a strawberry angel food cake. My mother admonished us three little girls to finish our breakfast and get dressed so we wouldn't be late for the picnic.

Odds on it is a beautiful day with a brilliantly clear sky so typical of an early summer day in North Dakota. (I didn't appreciate the sky then, because as a child I thought all skies looked that way. It was only after I had lived in other states and came back to visit that I realized a North Dakota sky has an incandescence all its own.) As we drive across the prairies the air is redolent with the scent of sweet-clover hay, which has just been taken in and which hangs loosely out from barn lofts. Early July was at once an enjoyable and an anxious time for my father and his neighbors. Enjoyable because the wheat had been planted and was waving green in the breeze, the hay safely in storage against the coming winter, and now there was a hiatus from work. Anxious because there seldom was enough rain—and would enough of it come in time to help the wheat before it began to ripen?

Driving along now, my father is in danger of going off the road, because he is judging his neighbors' fields as he drives and he looks in every direction except straight ahead. The field of wheat to his right, in his opinion, was planted too late; the one to his left was planted too early. *Look at that flax!* Someone has actually gambled eighty acres on a field of flax. Well, my father says, if the rains come his neighbor can make a fortune on *that* one. But it's chancy.

As we drive in to the Walstad brothers' farm where the picnic is being held, other automobiles brimming with children are also driving in. The farm is one of the most picturesque in the township. The small prairie-style house with its low-gabled roof sits on a hill with a small grove of cottonwood trees. At the bottom of the hill are the barns around which cattle and horses are milling, and halfway up the hill, ingeniously built into one side, is the ice house, the sine qua non of this Independence Day celebration.

We children tumble out of the cars screaming and laughing excitedly as we greet each other, and the women and older girls carry into the house their baskets filled with jars of ice cream makings and other food. They are greeted by Gunilla, a squat sweet-faced widow with a high chattery voice, who lives now with her two sons and an aged maiden aunt on this farm she homesteaded with her husband in the early 1900s. The women affectionately greet the plump ruddy-faced aunt, Kristina, whom everyone calls Tante; she customarily holds court from a high-backed rocker in the corner of the kitchen.

Outside, the men start down the hill to greet the Walstad brothers, Teddy and Hiram, who are walking up from the ice house with two tremendous burlap bags of ice on their backs for the great wooden freezer that stands in readiness at the top of the hill. They are handsome young men—giants, both of them—towering over most of the other men. Teddy (whom his mother calls Christopher, rolling the name out with great guttural $r$'s in the Norwegian manner) is a jovial bear of a man, with a great booming voice and laughter that rolls out of him like distant thunder. Hiram is even taller but slender and rather urbane; he wears steel-rimmed glasses and speaks softly. His wry sense of humor has a way of ambushing you from behind a dense blond mustache.

Teddy and Hiram were not only as likable a pair of brothers as you would want to meet, their neighbors said, but they were geniuses: whatever they set their minds on they could do. It was always pointed out, however, that Gunilla's bringing them up right didn't hurt. Gunilla's husband had died suddenly when the boys were teenagers, and she had forthwith turned the responsibility for the farm over to them. She didn't have a worry in the world,

*Nothing to Do but Stay*

she declared, because her boys, her *gutta,* would take care of everything. And they did. They soon proved to have an absolute flair for taking charge. Teddy was the more aggressive. He loved machinery and soon traded his draft horses for a tractor, his buggy for an automobile. He bought a threshing rig and harvested for his neighbors. He did custom feed-grinding. He acquired (of all things!) a typewriter. He kept meticulous records in a heavy ledger, a practice that bemused the other farmers, who mostly kept their records in their heads.

Hiram had a knack for animal husbandry and did veterinary work. He was a wizard at repairing watches and clocks. After he took a mail-order course in taxidermy, you never knew what might be staring down at you from the kitchen wall when you entered the Walstad house. Elk heads and stuffed owls competed for attention with birds popping out of cuckoo clocks, whose chimes were staggered to play in concert every hour on the hour.

There was another thing about Gunilla; she thought that all work and no play made dull *gutta.* She was all for her boys having some fun. She sent Teddy into the next township to take piano lessons from another homesteader, and soon he was playing beautiful organ music in church. He and Hiram, who fiddled by ear, teamed up and played for dances from one end of the township to the other.

And then there was the ice house. To have fun one must have quantities of good food, Gunilla always said, and that meant being able to have a dish or two of hand-cranked ice cream whenever one suddenly craved it. So—geniuses that they were—her *gutta* built a cunning ice house into the side of their hill, and in the cold winter months when there was little else to do, they took their ice saw down to the frozen Little Muddy Creek and laid in quantities of ice against the warm summer months.

This is why it is possible to have an ice cream social on this Fourth of July on the prairie. As Teddy and Hiram stagger up the hill now, with the ice on their backs, we children run behind, in front, and around them, screaming excitedly at the prospect of our first taste of ice cream since Christmas. Teddy takes an ax and pounds with the flat of it on the burlap sack to crush the ice. He shouts in the direction of the house that the women are holding him up on the makings.

Gunilla rushes out of the house, her face wreathed in smiles, carrying the steel freezer can of makings. She sets it carefully in the wooden shell of the freezer and returns to the house. We children crowd in to watch as Teddy and Hiram pack the freezer with ice, liberally sprinkling in layers of rock salt.

Now all of us smaller children are allowed a turn at cranking the freezer. As the handle begins to turn harder we are replaced with older children. Excitement mounts as the crank turns heavier, an indication that the magic taking place inside the steel container is working. Soon the older children yield their turns to the teenage boys, who grow red-faced as the cranking becomes more difficult.

"It won't be long now!" someone shouts.

A stout boy is chosen to sit on the freezer while Hiram makes the last difficult turns, a no-sweat grin lurking behind his mustache. The handle will no longer budge, the signal that the ice cream is indeed ready. We children giggle nervously as we hop around on one foot.

Teddy carefully removes the ice from the top of the container and a few inches below the steel cover. A sudden hush descends on the hill. The suspense is almost unbearable as the cover is lifted off to reveal the incredible frozen swirl beneath. A collective sigh of contentment wafts through the air. The first freezer of the day is the most thrilling one.

As a child I was part of this experience for a number of years before I could believe without a doubt that there *would* be ice cream under the cover. I don't know what I thought there would be—if not ice cream. But I felt that there could *possibly* be something else.

Teddy booms in the direction of the house, "Bring the saucers and spoons!" Several of the women rush out with the dishes and silverware. But something is missing. Again Teddy bellows toward the kitchen, "We need a scoop!"

Slowly out from the screen door emerges Tante, wad-dling with baby steps, her face flushed with excitement. She is carrying a long-handled wooden spoon. "Tante!" Teddy spreads his arms in mock surprise. "I knew you would save the day!" Everyone on the hill applauds. Her nephews adore her. She waddles back to the house.

We children line up for the first ice cream of the day. For many minutes nothing is heard except "Mmm" and "Aaah." This is what we have been anticipating for months. Hiram dips the long-handled spoon deeper and deeper into the freezer. Teddy shouts one more time at the house. "Bring your deepest platter!" On cue it is in-stantly forthcoming. The dasher is carefully lifted out onto the platter, and several lucky children are permitted to sit on the grass and scrape the ice cream off the beaters. The ice cream that comes off the dasher tastes the most deli-cious of all; some of the heaviest cream has congealed around it.

After the initial ice cream is eaten, it is time to take a break for lunch. Time to start the bonfire on which to roast the weiners. On a far corner of the hill small rocks have been placed in a circle to enclose the wood. The men take out their pocketknives and quickly strip the bark off some slender green cottonwood branches they cut from the nearby grove of trees to provide wands on which the children can place their weiners. The women bring out a dish towel–lined dishpan heaped with the fat brown buns which they have split and buttered, and we place our juicy charred weiners between them, then go in the house to fill our plates from the buffet the women have spread out in Gunilla's kitchen. It takes our breath away. Not so much the hot dishes and the salads, of which there are an abundance. But the cakes. One glorious cake after another lines the long table and overflows onto every available flat space in the kitchen. As my mother always said, "You bake what you have the ingredients for." And the ingredient every farmwife had at this time of the year was eggs. Every wife had at least two hundred chickens, at least half of them laying eggs at the onset of summer. Which meant that she was gathering at least a hundred eggs a day. Eggs were expendable. A dozen egg whites in a cake were nothing. Might as well make two or three. This is why Gunilla's kitchen is lined with cakes—every type of angel food, sponge, daffodil imaginable. A festival of cakes.

We children heap our plates and then take them out to the grove of cottonwood trees, under which have been placed wooden benches borrowed for the day from the country church a mile down the road. We are urged to go back for seconds and to take advantage of the waning fire to roast another weiner.

After lunch a somnolence gradually sifts down over the hill. It is time for the adults to *hvile middag*—to "rest dinner," the traditional Norwegian afternoon siesta. The women gather into groups on the wooden benches to drink coffee and chat, and the men lie on their backs on the grassy hill, chewing blades of grass and speculating whether the rains will come in time to save the wheat crop, their eyes following the cumulus clouds rolling past. My older sisters and the other teenage girls stroll up and down the hill in perfect step with each other, their arms entwined as they whisper delicious confidences. My brother Norman and the older boys try to organize a softball game in the flat of the meadow behind the barn, but it is a lethargic attempt, ending in a few fly balls being batted back and forth. We smaller children, who need anything but to "rest our dinners," race up and down the hill, playing tag, tackling each other, and seeing who can roll down the hill the fastest. We are marking time until this Fourth of July can get back on its track again—at which time the serious ice cream freezing and consumption will begin.

We giggle with joy when we see Teddy and Hiram and our fathers and all of the other men finally get off the grass and start down to the ice house. They bring enough ice up the hill to set two freezers going at once. And all through the long afternoon the men keep turning the cranks and producing one batch of ice cream after another, and we children keep lining up with our saucers and spoons. At four o'clock the women come out of the house to be served dainty dishes of ice cream to go along with their midafternoon cups of coffee. They urge us children to come in and sample some more of the cakes in which, they said, we scarcely made a dent.

As our bodies begin to throw grotesquely long shadows across the hill, we begin to feel that we may be reaching our limits of ice cream consumption. Teddy, waving his long-handled spoon in the air, is *begging* us to line up to have just one more dish. We are forced to decline; our tongues have become so coated with congealed ice cream that we lisp when we talk. We compare tongues to see who has been able to build up the most impressive deposit.

Looking at the sun suddenly dipping toward the horizon our parents announce that it is time to go home to milk the cows. The women gather up their baskets and put them into the automobiles along with their children, and thanks and good-byes are said.

But Teddy and Hiram have the last words. "Do you call *this* eating ice cream?" Teddy roars. "Come back this evening and we'll show you some *real* eating!"

"Better come back," Hiram coaxes softly, his eyes sparkling behind his steel rims. "It's a long time until Christmas."

Leaning out of the windows as the automobiles move down the lane toward home, we shake our heads in unison. At that moment, Christmas for once seems pleasingly far away.

# 7

# The Best of Both Worlds

Hvileløs *is the Norwegian word for restless. But rest-less* doesn't come within a mile of being as restless as *hvileløs*, which evokes someone who is fitty restless—as restless as a bewildered bedbug. Norwegians have a word for that, too: *forvirre veggelus*. Which, again, is ten times as bewildered as your average American bewildered bedbug.

This is by way of saying that Norwegian words convey, for me at least, an intensity of feeling that English words don't. Someone asks me in English, "What do you mean?" and that's all there is to it. "What do you mean?" But when someone asks me in Norwegian, "What mean you?" *Hva mener De?* it instantly suggests layers of implications, paving the way for going back generations if one cares to pursue it.

Growing up in a bilingual family meant that nothing ever had to suffer in translation. If restless wasn't restless enough for what we were describing, we could always use *hvileløs*. When it came to language, we had the best of both worlds.

From babyhood on up I heard two languages flowing in and out of each other as smoothly as two streams converging. My mother and father, who seemed to have an inviolable pact never to address each other except in the mother tongue, spoke to their children in either language, depending on how they were feeling at the time, and we invariably replied in English. This was not the case in most other families in our 100 percent Norwegian farm community. Many of the parents, fearful that their children would forget or even reject the language of the Old Country, insisted that their children address them in Norwegian. My mother and father didn't feel this way. Perhaps they were more liberal than their neighbors, or they simply might have felt that their six chattering children outnumbered them and it was or would very soon become a lost cause. At any rate, they were quite content to let us speak in English to them and to each other.

Early on, a bilingual child learns that each language has its own peculiar nuances. To me English seemed like an anemic and ineffectual language compared to the robust Norwegian. Stories told in Norwegian were funnier or sadder or grimmer. In our Norwegian Lutheran church a mile down the road, the minister preached three out of four sermons in Norwegian. The once-a-month English sermon didn't come near to raising the rafters as did the hellfire-and-brimstone sermons in Norwegian; those guttural Norse words with the rolling *r*'s could make you smell the fire and taste the brimstone. In casual conversation, even a mild invective in Norwegian would frighten me; a no-nonsense one—such as *"Fanden!"* The devil!—would set me to quivering. No English swearword seemed worthy of licking *fanden*'s bootstraps.

Although he was for the most part a quiet man, my father could tell a story like nobody's business. His stories were always wry and short. One reason they amused us so much was that they were usually a mixture of Norwegian and English. Among our favorites was the one about a newly married homesteader who came running across the prairies, blood rushing from his head, to wave down a neighbor plowing in his fields.

"Ivar, Ivar, come qvick!" he cried. "Geena hit me over the head with the *gryte*!"

If the homesteader had said kettle instead of *gryte*, the story wouldn't have been funny at all. But *gryte* was hilarious, made us roll on the floor.

Another favorite was about the man who reproved his

doltish son at the dinner table. The son was extending a long arm across the table to reach the dish of potatoes. The father cried out in Norwegian, "You should not sit there and fumble! You should say [switching to English], 'Please pass the *potet*!'"

Many of my father's stories came out of his childhood, which he painted as an idyllic time spent in eastern North Dakota's lush Red River valley. He was the penultimate child in a farm family of eight children. One story we loved was his recollection of the presidential election of 1896, when he was fifteen. His father, always intensely interested in politics, was a rabid William Jennings Bryan man. My father's uncle, who lived a few miles down the road, was for McKinley. Every evening before the election the uncle would come over, and the two men would argue themselves into a white heat. The rural elementary schoolteacher, who was boarding at the house that year, craved to enter the discussion, but the other two always spoke in Norwegian, which he didn't understand. The teacher finally got them to agree to speak only in English so he could join the debate. But when the argument reached the shouting stage, my father recalled with glee, his father and uncle would revert to Norwegian, leaving the schoolteacher high and dry and shaking with rage.

My father was a natural mimic, and he was never funnier than when he imitated the various brogues from the Old Country; the North Dakota homesteaders represented many of Norway's various counties and boroughs, all of which had their own peculiar dialect. My mother and father spoke Halling, because their parents had grown up in the Hallingdal valley. Many of our close neighbors were also Hallings; immigrants from the same place in Norway tended to band together in the new country. But in nearby townships there were also immigrants from Hardanger, Gudbransdal, Trondheim, Telemark, and Sogn. We thought those from Gudbransdal spoke rather formal and correct Norwegian, but the Telemarkings and particularly the Sognings had what sounded to us like deliciously ridiculous accents. When my father spoke Sogning, a fast, clipped, very know-it-all brogue, we collapsed into fits of laughter.

◆

I loved to sit in a corner of the kitchen and listen to the Norwegian dialogue when neighbors dropped in for a visit. My parents had known all of their neighbors since home-steading days; they had been through a lot together, and the bonds between them were strong. Reminiscences abounded. Even during the gloomiest years of the Dust Bowl they didn't sit around lamenting their fate. They took the position that this was a fallow period in their lives that had to be waited out, and they might as well accept it with good grace. They could always find something to laugh about. My mother and the other women would discuss the prolificacy of their laying hens and compare the egg prices (ten to fifteen cents a dozen) they had received that week in trade for groceries in Williston markets. The men would talk politics. They would speculate on what the *add*ministration, as they called it, was planning to do next to come to the aid of the "busted" farmers. Sprinkled through the Norwegian dialogue were the English words commodities, parity, mortgage, foreclosure, moratorium, and Nonpartisan League. Every man knew how his neighbor was going to vote in the next election—unless he was a "Langerman." The men who supported the notorious "Wild Bill" Langer, who raged through state politics in the thirties and forties like a North Dakota blizzard, tended to play it close to the chest.

After the egg prices and the state of the union had been disposed of, the conversation would take a more personal turn. This is the part I enjoyed the most: the part about who was currently keeping company with whom. In Norwegian it was a lot funnier than that. It was, literally, who was "driving on" whom. *Kjøre på*. Melvin *kjøre på* Clara. Melvin is driving on Clara. See, he was driving her around in an automobile. *Kjøre på* was a somewhat macho expression, often used by the men in a casual way to indicate a burgeoning romance. The women didn't use it so often. They were fonder of another expression. *Hun gå i giftetanke*. She goes in wedding thoughts. This indicated that a young person, most frequently a female, grew absent-minded and couldn't keep her mind on her work.

When someone, usually a man, got married to a stranger outside of the community, they said, *"Bjern har giftet seg."* Bjern has married himself. This confused me for years when I was a little girl. How could a man marry himself?

◆

The homesteaders, who had already been through one war a decade after settling into their new land, were just beginning to climb out of the Dust Bowl when suddenly they had World War II to worry about. Most of them had sons on one battlefield or another. Norman, a fighter pilot in the Burma-India theater of war, had been shot down once but managed to make his way back to his base. He was never far from my parents' thoughts. My father would time his farm chores so that he would always arrive back in the house before the next radio newscast. His favorite was Gabriel Heatter's fifteen-minute broadcast at 5:45 P.M. In order not to miss a word of it he would turn the radio on at 5:40, which meant he had to listen to the last five minutes of Wayne King and his orchestra, who were sponsored by Lady Esther cosmetics. Night after night my father would sit in his rocker in front of the radio, his face impassive as the dramatic cold-cream commercials promising more ethereal beauty in just ten days floated through

*My parents' North Dakota farm. The small unpainted buildings behind the house are my parents' homestead cabins. Photo by Adolph Lysne.*

the living room. He himself thought the radio had just two purposes: to report the news and to give the grain markets. Looking at my father staring into space as the mellifluous voice of the Lady Esther pitchman glided through the loudspeaker, I would have sworn that he had tuned this nonsense out so thoroughly he was hearing nothing.

*Nothing to Do but Stay*

One afternoon, however, he happened to glance out of the window and see a neighbor woman trudging down the road toward our farm. She was the slattern of the neighborhood—the *sjusket kvinne*—who didn't in any way resemble the other homesteaders' wives, most of whom were indefatigable, incredibly efficient women who worked as a matter of course from sunup to sundown. This woman had obviously arrived on the prairies by some terrible mistake or an ironical twist of fate. She was an execrable housekeeper, never cooked a decent meal, and weighed three hundred pounds. Her thin nervous husband, who labored constantly in his fields—probably to delay the awful hour when he must return to his house— had died after a few years, and she continued to live on the farm, renting out her land on cropshares and doing absolutely nothing. Every morning the weather permitted in spring, summer, and fall, she hit the road walking, swathed in a shapeless cotton dress, her placid wart-covered face set deep into her thick neck, her arms folded over her chest like a great buddha, marching from one end of the township to the other, "visiting" farm after farm, and always arriving at mealtime. Unless her timing was off, she could get in four square Norwegian meals a day—the hearty midmorning lunch, the noon dinner, the midafternoon bread-and-butter coffee break, and, on the way home, the substantial supper.

When my father, sitting out the cold-cream commercial

on this particular day of the last summer of World War II, saw this woman veering to leeward preparatory to turning her considerable bulk into our lane, his expression remained perfectly blank as he called out in Norwegian to my mother, who was in the kitchen preparing supper. "Set another plate. Here comes Lady Esther!"

# 8

## Thanks for the Last

Takk for sist *is a Norwegian phrase that means, liter-*
ally, thanks for the last and is what my mother always said
when greeting holiday guests at the door. It is a Norwegian's gracious way of saying, "What a fine time we had at
your house last time, and we hope you will find as much
joy in our home today."

In our Norwegian-American community, Christmas and
Thanksgiving were the great feast holidays; there was
rarely any entertaining by invitation at other times of the
year. If friends or relatives invited us for Thanksgiving, we
asked them back during Christmas week, or vice versa.

These winter holidays were feasts in every sense of the

word, whether they were at our farm or someone else's. The feasts began at high noon and ended at midnight. The big dinner, *middag*, was served in the middle of the day. At approaching dusk, the men guests—the husbands and sons—hurried home to milk the cows and feed the other livestock, driving as far as fifteen or twenty miles on snowy country roads in order to arrive back in time for a festive supper. Just before midnight everyone gathered around the table for the last time to sample the special holiday breads, cakes, and cookies that might have been passed up the first or second time around. At the stroke of twelve, drowsy children were collected from various parts of the house, the guests took a head count of those who belonged to them, and the children were bundled up and stowed into the automobile for the cold moonlit ride home across the prairies.

We often spent Thanksgiving at the Lundstroms, and they came back to our house during Christmas week. We seldom saw them at other times of the year. They lived on a farm about twelve miles across the prairies the way the crow flies. My father had an almost lyrical devotion to Hans Lundstrom because in the early 1900s he and Hans as young men in their twenties had homesteaded on adjacent quarters of land. They had both been carefree bachelors living in bare-bones style in their tiny homestead cabins, boiling coffee in tin cans on their potbellied stoves, existing in the winter on hardtack and jerky and in the summer sharing a garden of potatoes, turnips, and rutabagas—the only vegetables that either of them considered worth eating.

After my father married and moved his cabin to my mother's homestead, going to spend a holiday with the Lundstroms was always an emotional trip back in time for him; it gave him an excuse to drive past his old homestead —which someone else now owned but which, strangely, no one else had ever lived on. My father would stop the car along the road for a few minutes to survey the 160 acres of gently rolling prairies where he had first put down roots in western North Dakota, and his eyes would sweep over the land. The only identifying spot was a small but thick and perfectly round grove of box elder trees that my father had planted. The federal government had given every homesteader a packet of tree seeds to plant in order to beautify the land and also to provide a windbreak. Most of the homesteaders had providently spaced out their seeds evenly and carefully to the north and west of their homesites to shelter their buildings from the harsh northwest winds that blew down from Canada.

But it was easy to see—as we sat at the roadside twenty years later—that this was not what my father had done with his government seeds. Believing that a man should be able to see the horizon from every direction, he was not fond of trees, and one day he had impatiently spread the seeds round and round in a circle until he was rid of them.

Even now my father had no interest in trees. He wanted only to check the depth of the snow in the hollows and to determine whether the present owner had done any summer fallowing after harvest. As we sat there watching our father look at his homestead land, we all knew what he was thinking: it seemed only yesterday he was living on this land as a carefree young man, and today he was sitting looking at it with a wife and six children! But my father was, above all, a practical man, and the nostalgia lasted just a moment before he started up the car and we were moving again.

I loved going to the Lundstroms. They were Swedish, and Sophie Lundstrom had the reputation for setting one of the most fabulous tables in the county. Most of the Scandinavian homesteaders in northwestern North Dakota were Norwegians. We knew only a few Swedes and Danes. There was a much quoted adage, always spoken ironically and accompanied by plenty of laughter: Norwegians run deep, Danes run merry, and Swedes run best. It did seem that the Swedes we knew were natural achievers, whether at farming, housekeeping, or just being able to live a satisfying life.

Mrs. Lundstrom greeted us at the door with *"Tack for sist!"* and then the wholesale handshaking began. First the adults shook hands with the adults, then the adults shook hands with the children, and then the children shook hands with the children. My two eldest sisters, Bar-

ney and Florence, shook hands with the two oldest Lundstrom daughters, Lillian and Clara. My brother Norman
shook hands with Eric Lundstrom. And then we three little girls—Gladys and Fran and I—shook hands with little
Tina Lundstrom, which ended in a fit of giggles, and we
had to be admonished.

Now came the time that my father dreaded: waiting for
dinner to be served. All good Scandinavians in the territory had their holiday dinners at high noon. Mrs. Lundstrom always asked us for twelve o'clock, so, like good
guests, we were always there before the stroke of twelve.
But years of experience told my father that it would be at
least 1:30 and possibly, God forbid, even two o'clock before Sophie Lundstrom would have dinner on the table.
My father was a punctual man. At the top of his code of
ethics was "Be on time!" And being on time meant that
meals should be served at the proper hour. If my father
had the choice of eating meagerly and promptly or sump-
tuously an hour late, he would take short rations every
time. But here in the house of his dearest friend there was
nothing to do but wait.

Mrs. Lundstrom seated us in the parlor. My mother and
older sisters sat on the leather davenport and looked at
photograph albums. My brother Norman amused himself
on a leather rocker with a wondrous loose back that
flopped over on him when he leaned forward. Gladys and
Fran and I sat on the piano bench. We couldn't play with

the Lundstrom children because their mother had them marshaled like a platoon carrying things back and forth from the kitchen to the dining room. My father and Hans Lundstrom sat across from each other, each on his own deacon's bench, and recalled their bachelor homesteading days from start to finish—including the story about the homesteader's wife who sold them bread so hard they had to cut it with a carpenter's saw. The grandfather clock struck one o'clock, then 1:15. My father began to rub his hand across his face—a gesture we knew was the sign of last endurance—and we three little girls squirmed uneasily on the piano bench. At times like this he had been known to bolt—after suddenly remembering a sick cow that needed immediate attention at home.

After my father had crossed and uncrossed his legs for what I thought must be the thousandth time, the clock struck 1:30 and Mrs. Lundstrom miraculously appeared at the door, her face moist and ruddy from hours over the hot stove. She gestured toward the dining room. *"Var så god!"* she said—the traditional words that meant, "Please honor us by accepting what we have to offer."

The first sight of Sophie Lundstrom's dinner table always made me gasp. It completely filled the long narrow dining room, whose south windows opened out on a sunporch beyond which one could see miles of snow-covered

*Nothing to Do but Stay*

prairies reflecting the sun. Places were laid for fourteen with white china on a white damask tablecloth. There was no color on the table at all except a luscious ribbon of translucent jellies, relishes, and preserves that ran down the length of the table and caught up the sun—like a feast spread out in the snow. In the center was a glorious crown tomato aspic, and streaming down on either side were grape and chokecherry jellies, rhubarb jam and plum preserves, pickled beets, spiced crabapples, and watermelon pickles.

After we were all seated and Hans Lundstrom had said grace, the older Lundstrom daughters took up their stands at each end of the table to help pass the dishes and to take them away. Mrs. Lundstrom disappeared into the kitchen. She reappeared a moment later triumphantly bearing the *pièce d'occasion*, a tremendous silver platter of diaphanous steamed *lutefisk*. It was glistening with drawn butter.

*"Var så god!"* Mrs. Lundstrom said, offering the dish first to my mother.

When the *lutefisk* came around to me, I put as small a portion as I could on my plate without attracting attention to myself. But I helped myself liberally to the *lefse,* which Clara Lundstrom was offering on a round blue-and-white china platter. The perfectly baked, pale-flecked pieces of potato pancake had been buttered and folded into tricorns, then artfully arranged, layer upon layer in circles around the platter.

Then, in a steady procession, came mashed potatoes topped with melting butter and paprika, a tureen of Swedish meatballs (*köttbullar*), carrots and peas in cream, and my favorite—scalloped corn. I could have made a meal of Mrs. Lundstrom's scalloped corn alone. Fragrant with onion, it was baked until it was quite dry and very chewy. The casserole was always served in a fancy filigreed silver holder with mahogany handles.

After our plates were so heaped that there was room for nothing more, we ate steadily for a few minutes. But when Mrs. Lundstrom observed that we were making slight inroads into our plates, she began to pass around the compote dishes that ran down the center of the table. First the tomato aspic and then all of the jams, jellies, preserves, and pickles. My father never failed to mutter about this on our way home. He always said, "Sophie didn't give me a chance to eat. I never got a piece of *lutefisk* to my mouth but what I had to pass the pickles."

The truth is that my father after a certain length of time at the dinner table became so weary of passing dishes that when they came to him he would simply set them down again in the center of the table in the hope of cutting off the flow. But after a few minutes the eagle-eyed Sophie, hovering behind his chair, would reach a discreet arm in and start them on their way again.

Trying to finish everything on my plate so as not to disgrace my mother, I had conflicting emotions: joyful anticipation of dessert and fear that I was not going to have room for it. One thing in my favor was that there would be at least a forty-five-minute wait for dessert. When Mrs. Lundstrom cleared the table, she meant clear the table. Everything came off, including all of the compote dishes, and if someone's hand had slipped and dropped a bit of plum jelly, the damask tablecloth would come off, too, and a fresh one laid. It took time to replace and refill fourteen water glasses and serve the coffee. I was grateful for this delaying action—until I looked at my father. He looked as if he were about to conjure up an emergency at home and take flight. But just at that moment Mrs. Lundstrom came in proudly bearing the first plate of dessert. She placed it in front of my mother.

*"Var så god!"* she beamed.

It was hazelnut meringue cake, with a scoop of hand-cranked chocolate ice cream.

My mouth watered with delight; at the same time I inwardly moaned that I would never be able to finish it all. My mother said, "You must give the little girls only half a portion, Sophie." I was saved.

When dessert was finished and the plates removed, my father, believing now that there was real hope for escape, became quite cheerful—until the Lundstrom daughters came in with clean dessert plates and set them around! My father looked absolutely stricken; he had forgotten about the last course. Now came the promenade of the fancy Scandinavian cookies: the *fattigman,* the *pepparkakor,* the *krumkaker,* the *berlinerkranzer,* and the *sandbak-kels.* The only one at the table who could eat a cookie was Norman, who took two and polished them off. Everyone stared at him in wonder and admiration. There was a twelve-year-old boy for you.

As we left the table, we filed past Mrs. Lundstrom and thanked her, *"Takk for maten."* She replied, *"Vel-bekomme."*

Having earned her rest, Mrs. Lundstrom settled down with my mother for a cozy chat in the corner of the kitchen where she could keep an eye on her older daughters and my older sisters while they washed the dishes. My father and Hans Lundstrom, neither of whom smoked except on holidays, had a Thanksgiving cigar in the living room.

We younger children went outdoors to play, and Eric took us into the big red barn for a ride on the manure carrier—one of the great thrills of the day for me. This strange piece of equipment, built like a huge whale, hung suspended from poles that ran up into a track in the low ceiling of the barn, somewhat like the horses in a merry-go-round. Like everything else at the Lundstroms, it looked as if it had just been scrubbed. I never could figure out where the manure came in or where it went out; it

*Nothing to Do but Stay*

seemed perfectly seamless, and there was no manure in evidence anywhere. I think it must have been one of Hans Lundstrom's ingenious inventions, because I played in a lot of barns in the course of my childhood and I never saw another one like it. Eric let us ride two at a time, each hanging on to a pole. Starting at the front end of the barn, he scooted the carrier on the track all along the length of the barn and then out the back door where the track extended several yards out into the barnyard. As we streaked smoothly through the interior of the dark barn and then suddenly emerged into the bright sunlight, it was almost like being shot out of a cannon. It was scary, and we screamed at the top of our lungs. Little Tina Lundstrom screamed louder than any of us. "Just one more time, Eric," she pleaded.

But Eric could only be talked into a certain number of rides. As we came out to play in the snow, the sun suddenly disappeared as if someone had dropped it behind the grove of box elder trees that lined the western edge of the farm. At the same moment my father rushed out of the house and shouted to Norman that the two of them had to hurry home to milk the cows. The rest of us children went back into the house. Eric, having lost his friend for a couple of hours, decided to amuse us little girls by telling us stories. We went upstairs and sat on the floor in the square hallway, and Eric pretended to be a very, very old Scandinavian pioneer. He cupped his chin in his hand and brought it down across his chest as if he were pulling on a long white beard, and then in the most preposterous Swedish brogue he made up wild stories of how he "koom over from the Ewld Coontry," took a "hewmstead," was attacked by buffalo, bushwacked by coyotes, and lost in blizzards. We laughed until our sides ached. Tina Lundstrom laughed harder than any of us. Like the ride on the manure carrier, these stories seemed to come out of Eric only at Thanksgiving.

We heard dishes clattering in the kitchen, and I was surprised that I was feeling hungry again. Eric went out to help his father milk the cows, and we four little girls wandered around upstairs and into a bedroom where Lillian and Clara Lundstrom were showing my older sisters their hope chests. The two great chests, lids opened against the wall, gave out the pungent odor of fresh cedar. Each chest contained three double-damask tablecloths and three dozen napkins, a dozen percale sheets and pillowcases crocheted around the edges, four dozen linen dish towels, and a handstitched quilt in the wedding ring pattern.

Mrs. Lundstrom's voice came up the stairwell, calling for her daughters to come down and help get supper on the table. Hans Lundstrom came in from doing the chores and lighted the gas lamp. We had one like it at home that we used only for special occasions. It had two filamented net mantles which were fastened over the gas jets and which had to be generated several minutes with kitchen matches before the jets were released. If the mantles weren't heated the proper length of time, the lamp would puff and act up. But when the lamp was finally adjusted and turned up to its maximum intensity, it gave an incredibly beautiful bright white incandescent light. Hans Lundstrom hung the lamp on a great hook on the ceiling of the parlor. Then he lighted the kerosene lamps that sat in sconces along the walls in the kitchen and dining room. Their amber lights, with reflected glory from the gas lamp in the parlor, gave the house a soft enchantment. My mother sat in the kitchen and chatted with Mrs. Lundstrom as she prepared supper. Suddenly sleepy, I put my head in my mother's lap and dozed. Soon we saw automobile lights coming up the lane; my father and Norman were returning from doing the chores at home.

Now we were gathered around the dining room table again, everyone relaxed and happy in the glow of evening. Our supper was basically a *koldtbord,* a cold table, with two kinds of cold sliced meat, one a spicy beef roll called *rullpölsa* and the other a rather bland pressed pork roll, *sylta,* which was especially good with pickled beets. We also had potato salad and two kinds of bread, *rågbröd* (a Swedish rye redolent of orange) and a crusty cinnamon-raisin bread, along with another chance at all of the preserves and relishes.

The unforgettable part of the supper—one that I would dream about from one holiday to the next—was a glorious apple salad in a magnificent cut-glass bowl that was deeply scalloped around the edge. Chopped apples and whole marshmallows were folded into mountains of whipped cream, and the peaks were sprinkled with almonds. I thought it was the most beautiful sight I had ever seen; it tasted and looked the way I imagined manna from heaven. For dessert, there was sponge cake sprinkled with confectioner's sugar and the remainder of the chocolate ice cream. I decided I liked Thanksgiving suppers the best of all.

While the Lundstrom daughters and my sisters cleared the table and washed the dishes, Mrs. Lundstrom and my mother went to sit in the downstairs bedroom for a last minute chat; they had a year's events to catch up on. We four little girls went upstairs to sit in the hallway and play Uncle Wiggly and Old Maid. We could hear Eric and Norman in the next room talking seriously about their plans to trap badgers and weasels and collect the bounty. My father and Hans Lundstrom had a last cigar in the parlor; the fragrant smoke wafted up the stairwell.

"Time to go home!" My father was calling to us from the bottom of the stairs.

"No! No!" Mrs. Lundstrom cried. "First we must have something to eat."

The coffee pot was set to boiling on the stove, and the Lundstrom daughters were set to work again. In a few minutes we were sitting around the table eating bread and butter and all of the fancy cookies we had passed up at dinner. This time I managed to sample most of them.

The clock was striking midnight as we bundled into our winter coats and stocking caps and boots. Everyone shook hands again all around. *"Tusen takk. Det var så moro,"* my mother said. A thousand thanks. It was such fun. As we climbed into the car, she called out, "Now do not forget! You are coming to us Christmas week."

On the long drive home through the snow, I sat in my mother's lap in the front seat. Fran was snuggled down between my mother and father. My three other sisters and Norman dozed in the back seat. The snow made a crisp sound under the automobile tires, and occasionally a jack-rabbit scurried across the road.

Suddenly my father shouted, "Wake up, children! Northern lights!"

We were driving north, and ahead of us, low in the sky, were luminous lights that glowed for a moment, then faded, then glowed again as if a great hand were turning them up and down.

"We don't need to go to the Old Country tonight to see the fireworks," my father said fiercely. It was a point of pride with the homesteaders that northwestern North Dakota, because of its high latitude, often had spectacular aurora borealis reminiscent of those over Norway.

My mother's thoughts were elsewhere. "Have you ever tasted such food?" she said dreamily.

"Sophie Lundstrom is a fine cook, all right," my father conceded, swerving to avoid another rabbit caught in the glare of the headlights. "But I don't know why, just when I am setting to and enjoying the *lutefisk* and *lefse,* that she has to have all of that passing from hand to hand. All those jellies and jams and all those things. It doesn't give a man a chance to enjoy his food."

My mother was silent. My father turned to look at her for a moment and then burst out accusingly, "But I don't know why I should talk like this about Sophie. When they come to us Christmas week you will be doing exactly the same thing!"

My mother pursed her lips, turned away from my father, and looked defiantly out of the window at the snow-covered prairies rolling past.

"People have to *eat,*" she said.